"Chris Rice and Emmanuel Katongole know how much genuine reconciliation costs; therefore, they are perfect leaders to teach us not to take the task too lightly or to try to bring it about too superficially. This is a critically important book and an incisive beginning to what promises to be a world-changing series. Christians have a unique vision to live—the new creation of whole-hearted community!"

Marva J. Dawn, teaching fellow in spiritual theology, Regent College, and author of *Truly the Community, Unfettered Hope* and *My Soul Waits*

"Rather than suggesting formulaic or easy steps, Father Emmanuel Katongole and Chris Rice challenge their readers to embody a spirituality that reconciles. With the compelling texture of real-life stories, the credibility of their own journeys in reconciliation, and humble yet profound theological reflections, Emmanuel and Chris offer an accessible and fresh entry point for the crucial conversations on reconciliation."

Christopher L. Heuertz, international executive director, Word Made Flesh, and author of *Simple Spirituality*

"My only concern is that not enough people will read this fine book! Given how much humans let things fall apart, this resource is a gem for individuals, groups and institutions. Is there a future for us if we do not learn exactly *how* to heal and reconcile?"

Richard Rohr, O.F.M., Center for Action and Contemplation, Albuquerque, New Mexico

"*Reconciling All Things* is a faithful book, glowing with the joy and hope that come from walking with God and God's people in the world. Inviting all to join in God's reconciling work across the myriads of ways we live in brokenness, Katongole and Rice do a new thing—they retrieve a deeply theological vision of God's gift of reconciliation and show what the inbreaking of this gift looks like in the real stories of people who have embarked on this journey. These stories of pain and hope make clear that the real work of reconciliation is not as much about programs, strategies or fixing all things as it is about the ordinary, mundane, daily work of living faithfully and patiently in our local, particular, face-to-face contexts. And if we do, if we enter humbly into God's work in the world, what can happen? New creation!"

M. Therese Lysaught, associate professor and assistant chair, Department of Theology, Marquette University

"This is a tough and a hopeful book. Tough, not because it is hard to read, but because it calls us to what the authors portray as the imperative but long, painful and not always rewarding journey of reconciliation. But hopeful because it is full of keen insights, fascinating stories and wise counsel. If we truly believe God is in Christ reconciling the world to himself, then this book is important reading. Read it and heed the call to join in God's great story of reconciliation. You will find yourself both challenged beyond comfort, yet moved with great expectations."

Leighton Ford, president, Leighton Ford Ministries, Charlotte, North Carolina USA, and author of *Transforming Leadership* and *The Attentive Life*

Reconciling
ALL THINGS

A Christian Vision for Justice, Peace and Healing

EMMANUEL KATONGOLE
& CHRIS RICE

Resources for Reconciliation

series editors

EMMANUEL KATONGOLE AND CHRIS RICE

IVP Books
An imprint of InterVarsity Press
Downers Grove, Illinois

InterVarsity Press
P.O. Box 1400, Downers Grove, IL 60515-1426
World Wide Web: www.ivpress.com
E-mail: email@ivpress.com

InterVarsity Press® is the book-publishing division of InterVarsity Christian Fellowship/USA®, a student movement active on campus at hundreds of universities, colleges and schools of nursing in the United States of America, and a member movement of the International Fellowship of Evangelical Students. For information about local and regional activities, write Public Relations Dept., InterVarsity Christian Fellowship/USA, 6400 Schroeder Rd., P.O. Box 7895, Madison, WI 53707-7895, or visit the IVCF website at <www.intervarsity.org>.

All Scripture quotations, unless otherwise indicated, are taken from the New American Standard Bible®, copyright 1960, 1962, 1963, 1968, 1971, 1972, 1973, 1975, 1977, 1995 by The Lockman Foundation. Used by permission.

Design: Rebecca Larson

Images: Veer

ISBN 978-0-8308-3451-8

Printed in the United States of America ∞

Library of Congress Cataloging-in-Publication Data

Katongole, Emmanuel, 1960-
  Reconciling all things: a Christian vision for justice, peace, and
healing / Emmanuel Katongole and Chris Rice.
     p. cm.—(Resources for reconciliation)
  Includes bibliographical references.
  ISBN 978-0-8308-3451-8 (pbk.: alk. paper)
  1. Reconciliation—Religious aspects—Christianity. I. Rice, Chris,
  1960- II. Title.
  BT738.27.K38 2008
  234'.5-dc22

                                                                          2008022667

P	20	19	18	17	16	15	14	13	12	11	10	9	8	7	6	5	4	3	2	1
Y	25	24	23	22	21	20	19	18	17	16	15	14	13	12	11	10	09	08

Dedicated to

John Perkins of Mississippi

and

Cardinal Emmanuel Wamala of Uganda,

everyday saints

who have shown us the way

Contents

SERIES PREFACE 9

INTRODUCTION 11

1 Prevailing Visions of Reconciliation 21

2 Stepping Back: Reconciliation as the Goal of God's Story. . 39

3 Reconciliation Is a Journey with God 47

4 How Scripture Reshapes Us. 57

5 The Discipline of Lament 75

6 Hope in a Broken World 95

7 Why Reconciliation Needs the Church 109

8 The Heart, Spirit and Life of Leadership. 123

EPILOGUE: *Going the Long Haul* 143

RECOVERING RECONCILIATION AS THE MISSION OF GOD
Ten Theses. 147

ACKNOWLEDGMENTS 153

Recommended Resources 155

Notes 159

About the Authors 161

About the Duke Divinity School Center
for Reconciliation 163

About Resources for Reconciliation 167

Series Preface

The Resources for Reconciliation Book Series

A partnership between InterVarsity Press and the Center for Reconciliation at Duke Divinity School, Resources for Reconciliation books address what it means to pursue hope in areas of brokenness, including the family, the city, the poor, the disabled, Christianity and Islam, racial and ethnic divisions, violent conflicts and the environment. The series seeks to offer a fresh and distinctive vision for reconciliation as God's mission and a journey toward God's new creation in Christ. Each book is authored by two leading voices, one in the field of practice or grassroots experience, the other from the academy. Each book is grounded in the biblical story, engages stories and places of pain and hope, and seeks to help readers to live faithfully—a rich mix of theology, context and practice.

This book series was born out of the mission of the Duke Divinity School Center for Reconciliation: *Advancing God's mission of reconciliation in a divided world by cultivating new leaders, communicating wisdom and hope, and connecting in outreach to strengthen leadership.* A divided world needs people with the vision, spiritual maturity and daily skills integral to reconciliation. The church needs fresh resources—a mix of biblical vision, skills in social and historical analysis, and practical gifts of spirituality and social leadership—in order to pursue reconciliation in real places, from congregations to communities.

The ministry of reconciliation is not reserved for experts. It is the core of God's mission and an everyday call of the Christian life. These books are written to equip and stimulate God's people to be more faithful ambassadors of reconciliation in a fractured world.

For more information, email the Duke Divinity School Center for Reconciliation at reconciliation@div.duke.edu, or visit our website: <http://www.divinity.duke.edu/reconciliation/>.

Emmanuel Katongole
Chris Rice
Center codirectors and series editors

Introduction

Reconciling All Things. It's a pretty preposterous title for a book. Especially one as short as this. If the title is ambitious, it is because this book arises out of our deep restlessness about what it means to live faithfully in a broken and divided world.

One of us is American. One of us is African. One is Protestant, one Catholic. One is a practitioner, one a theologian. Yet our journeys cross and defy easy categories, borders and loyalties. We find ourselves bound together as restless pilgrims in search of something better in a divided world.

The restlessness and convictions of this book grow out of three pilgrim journeys.

A PILGRIM'S LIFE

For me (Chris), even after seven years in Durham, North Carolina, I still feel like a stranger in unfamiliar territory. I am as white and American as most of my dear friends at Blacknall Presbyterian Church. My children play in soccer leagues and ride horses. We live in a quiet and stable urban neighborhood. Trained at Duke Divinity School, where I now serve, I can talk the talk of the academic world.

But the most important education I ever received came during my twelve years growing up in South Korea as a son of missionary parents and my seventeen years living in an inner-city black neighborhood in Jackson, Mississippi. There I was, born in the U.S.A. but growing up in bustling Seoul during the tumultuous post-Korean war years, when we also saw an explosive growth of Christianity. And there I was after that, studying Chinese at Middlebury College and aspiring to a government career. I took a summer break to volunteer in Mississippi, of all places.

I arrived in Mississippi in 1981 as a starry-eyed twenty-one-year-old. There at Voice of Calvary Ministries—founded by Mississippi pastor and activist John Perkins in an inner-city neighborhood that had been abandoned by churches of every color—Christians of different races worshiped, worked and lived side-by-side on the same streets, seven days a week. You name it, Voice of Calvary did it: housing, economic development, youth ministry. It was an exciting place to be.

I went to Jackson for three months and stayed for seventeen years. My wife, Donna, and I met and married at Voice of Calvary, and our three children were all born or adopted there. I saw our church almost split over a racial crisis. I experienced revelations of how God can bring joy, friendship and new life out of pain, failure and weakness. Along the way, I became an unlikely friend and colaborer with Spencer Perkins, the founder's son, who grew up amid intense racial animosity. We helped start a Christian community called Antioch, where our families lived for twelve years. We also founded a national reconciliation ministry and wrote a book to tell our story.

Then Spencer and I nearly split apart in 1997—a bitter relational crisis. Yet somehow, with the help of friends, we learned to give each other enough grace to go on and to trust God for the lack. Just trying to live peacefully in one neighborhood, in one church and with one person named Spencer taught me that reconciliation is a long and fragile journey.

But the most important lesson of those seventeen Mississippi years was this: even in a deeply divided world, even in the most deeply divided relationship, *the way things are is not the way things have to be.*

After Spencer's sudden death in 1998 and a period of discernment, our family opened a new chapter. Here in a different place—on the other side of the tracks at Duke University—I found myself immediately restless: can places like Duke and West Jackson say hello, become friends and transform each other?

Through this pilgrimage from America to Korea to Mississippi to Duke, I find myself constantly longing and searching for communion across worlds and divides I have lived on both sides of—Asia and America, black and white, haves and have-nots, action and reflection, Blacknall's Presbyterian deliberateness and Voice of Calvary's gospel choir spontaneity, Korean *kimchi* and Mississippi ribs, the reality of West Jackson gunshots and the beauty of Duke gardens.

AFRICAN IN AMERICA

This book's second source of restlessness is found in Emmanuel's journey.

For me (Emmanuel) as well, this has been an unexpected pilgrim journey, for I never imagined myself at a place like Duke.

Here I am, a Ugandan who grew up in the small village of Malube. A Catholic priest in a Methodist seminary. An African living in the United States. I am a village-born-and-bred son of Uganda who can remember waking up to 5:00 a.m. chores in the garden before running the two miles to school. But I have also been able to study in Uganda, Rome and Belgium. I am now teaching in a wealthy research university, going home and back again and again in the name of a fresh conversation about Africa.

My father came from a poor family in Rwanda to Uganda, raising seven children with my mother. He never went to school himself yet became a parent leader at our school and mobilized children in the village to get an education. My father died when I was twelve. My brother died of AIDS in 1993. When civil war broke out in 1980, my mother fled the house as the military demolished every living thing. She walked fifty miles to Kampala and did not return until six years later. Here I am, with both my experience of growing up in Africa under the brutal regime of Idi Amin and my involvement in the dynamic and rich traditions of the African church.

In all my teaching I find myself in search of something better than the tribalization that divides so much of Africa, or categories such as North and South, black and white. Here I am, pressing the question as I teach, "But what does this theology mean for my mother?" What does it mean back in Malube, where trees are being cut down by powerful businesses, where roads are in disrepair, where clean water is not available, where the priest lives in a faraway town? What does it mean for our conversations about God and peace never to be disconnected from the challenges of real, local places, from digging wells, organizing education and planting trees?

Whether it is building community between African and American congregations through the ministry of Share the Blessings or leading pilgrimages of Duke students and faculty to Uganda or supporting Ugandans who serve as priests in American parishes, my life is about being at Duke and at the same time never leaving Africa.

A SHARED JOURNEY

The third source of restlessness for this book comes out of the journey we have shared.

We discovered each other in a classroom at Duke, Emmanuel as teacher and Chris as student. Soon we were friends, discovering we were even born the same year. Eventually a remarkable international journey merged with our two journeys through the Reconciliation Track of the 2004 Lausanne Forum for World Evangelization.

Chris was invited to convene the Reconciliation Track and invited Emmanuel to join the leadership team. The journey took the team to Duke, to Rwanda ten years after the genocide and to the October 2004 Thailand forum of 1,500 participants. Over that week in Thailand we joined fifty Christian leaders in our track from twenty-one of the world's most divided places historically—from Korea to Northern Ireland, from India to South Africa. As we worshiped across denominations and nations, ate together, debated and reflected on our ministries of reconciliation, something beautiful happened: strangers became companions, and a global community of the restless was born.

Rooming together in Thailand, the two of us bonded and talked into the night each evening. Returning to Duke, conversations intensified with Greg Jones, our dean, about a major new initiative focused on reconciliation. By December 2004, the two of us were walking down a North Carolina beach as the new codirectors of the Duke Center for Reconciliation, sharing our dreams for what a center would look like if it were to take seriously both social realities and Scripture, action and reflection, America and Africa. Yet even in this growing friendship, we weren't sure what we were getting into. As Protestant and Catholic in churches that do not share the Communion cup, we knew the church's brokenness was at the heart of our restlessness.

Since that walk in December 2004, we have walked together in one another's formative villages in Uganda and Mississippi. Chris saw the church where Emmanuel was baptized into the faith. Emmanuel saw the Antioch dinner table that bound Chris into a beloved community.

Now, three years into the journey of the center, a major new initiative is forming around reconciliation—a seedbed for future leaders (we send students to both Mississippi and Uganda), a resource center and a fueling station to nourish Christian leaders in America and across the world. Every semester is full of encounters—at Duke, across America and around the world—with people working in places of deep pain with great hope. We end every semester on that same North Carolina coast, walking the beach and naming the gifts. This journey is not worth it without joy and celebration along the way, without remembering the bigger story we are in.

THE CONVICTIONS IN THIS BOOK

The convictions we explore in this book became clear to us only as we worked together to establish the center. We discovered we had developed strong, common convictions about reconciliation as a Christian vision and practice.

Indeed, in our zest for constantly bridging diverse worlds, we see a bigger journey—a quest for God's new creation and a fresh vision for the church—neither the church of the current divides nor the church enmeshed in violence, but the church as it can be: the bride of Christ, drawn from every nation, tongue, tribe and denomination.

Many of our students and other Christian young people we meet are searching for such a fresh vision. They are eager to break the bubble of familiarity and comfort to serve in South Africa, Uganda, Sudan, Chicago, Washington, D.C., and Mississippi. They return very restless, and are never the same.

Yet reconciliation is not only for seminary students or ministry "professionals" or those who go far and wide in the name of peace. The basic conviction of this book is that reconciliation as a Christian vision makes a claim on the life of every person, place and congregation—it is not the terrain of experts and professionals. This book is for you, wherever you live.

This quest of everyday people for God's new creation in a broken world is the theme of the Resources for Reconciliation book series. In *Reconciling All Things,* the lead title, our intention is to trace the broad strokes of a journey of reconciliation that is distinctly Christian—a movement from seeing the story of Scripture, to learning to lament, to seeing what hope looks like in a broken world. We are not satisfied with the ways reconciliation is commonly approached within and beyond the church. So we begin by thinking critically about prevailing visions of reconciliation.

Two words are crucial throughout this book: *journey* and *gifts.* Reconciliation is indeed an invitation into a journey. It is not a "solution" or an end product, but a process and an ongoing search.

But we need gifts to engage this journey well. The good news of this book is that God has not left the world alone. God has given us everything we need to sustain us on the journey. One gift at the heart of this book is hope—a hope that flows from the conviction of our own life journeys: *the way things are is not the way things have to be.* Wherever we go in the most broken places of the world, God is always planting seeds of hope. This hope is often under the radar screen and easily missed. In this book we share stories of God's new creation breaking in, the good news of what the Holy Spirit is doing throughout the world.

We see profound hope in the lives of faithful people who have gone before us. So part of our methodology in this book is to illuminate the lives of key leaders in reconciliation and cull insights from their work. Thus we'll revisit certain examples throughout.

At the end of the book we propose ten theses for "Recovering Reconciliation as the Mission of God." Our hope is to provide a roadmap for the rest of the series, which will begin to fill out the "all things," exploring different aspects of the Christian vision of reconciliation in relationship to real problems and challenges.

BECOMING MORE CHRISTIAN

One of the journeys we shared was Duke Divinity School's 2005 Pilgrimage of Pain and Hope in Uganda and Rwanda. Over the course of our two-week journey, a highlight was our Kampala, Uganda, visit with Cardinal Emmanuel Wamala, one of Emmanuel's spiritual mentors.

Greeting us warmly in his white robe and red hat, Wamala spoke eloquently of the challenge of living faithfully. "We have the book," he said, speaking of Africans and the Bible. "But how much do we know about it?"

Later the cardinal joked with Dean Greg Jones that Duke should be canonized for putting up with Emmanuel for all these years. Then, reflecting on Emmanuel's presence as an African Catholic at this Protestant seminary in America, the cardinal offered striking words: "No, you have not made him more Catholic. You have made him more Christian."

In the end, learning to become faithful pilgrims amid the brokenness of this world is about becoming more Christian. A Rwandan proverb says, "To go fast, walk alone. To go far, walk together." When we learn how to slow down to make room for walking together across divides, we become more Christian.

That is what this book is about—becoming more Christian by slowing down.

I

Prevailing Visions of Reconciliation

*W*e live in a broken world. Start the day with the newspaper or start it with a quiet time, you'll soon come face to face with the sin that separates us from God and puts up walls between people. The brokenness of our world is more than a point of Christian doctrine. It is a reality that shapes our daily lives.

In 1964, in Trosly-Breuil, France, two men with mental disabilities woke up in an isolated institution, shut off from a world that had little time for them. Useless to the economy that determines success for most of us, these men were destined to be little more than the recipients of mental health services. Meanwhile, in the same French town, a former naval officer and promising young academic named Jean Vanier had just finished his doctoral dissertation. Although to all appearances successful, Vanier was lonely. Like the men in the mental institution, he was isolated and unsure whether anyone loved him for who he was. Vanier had no idea that he shared anything in common with men in a mental institution. Nothing had taught him to question society's division between "normal" people and the disabled.

In 1970 John Perkins, an African American pastor and community organizer who lived on "the black side" of rural Mendenhall, Mississippi, was nearly beaten to death by white state police officers. The Christianity that Perkins and the police officers shared did nothing to challenge the wall that racism had built between them. Indeed, in the aftermath of a brutal assault, Perkins could only hope that division would protect him from further violence. In the turmoil of 1970, he had good reason to want nothing to do with white people.

In 1974, Billy Neal Moore, an Army soldier at home on leave in Georgia, tried to rob seventy-seven-year-old Fred Stapton in his home. When Stapton heard an intruder, he shot into the darkness. Moore shot back and killed him. "When I found out that I had actually killed somebody, I couldn't believe it," Moore said. He pled guilty to the murder and was sentenced to death. Stapton's family had lost their father and grandfather; Moore had lost any hope of a future. Literal walls stood around Moore to ensure that he would never meet the people his actions had hurt. United by violence, Moore and his victim's family were divided by a society that could not imagine redemption.

In 1990, a white South African Anglican priest named Michael Lapsley, chaplain of the African National Congress at the time, opened a letter from forces inside the apartheid government. The bomb inside blew off his hands and an eye, shattering his eardrums. For years Lapsley had patiently worked for justice in his country, only to be betrayed by white South Africans who considered him a traitor. Lapsley had tried to cross a dividing line and had come face to face with the power of division. Was he too idealistic, imagining that South Africa could move beyond apartheid to become a society that embraced white and black as equals?

In northern Uganda, where families live in fear inside one of the world's most pressing (and least talked about) situations of violence, 139 children were abducted from their school by the Lord's Resistance Army in 1996. The children included the fourteen-year-old daughter of Angelina Atyam, a midwife and nurse. Atyam knew she would never see her daughter again. Thousands of parents before her had bitterly resigned themselves to a brutal reality that could not be changed. She had every reason to be angry, but little room to hope that anything could change.

Though not all of us have experienced the large-scale trauma of war or the violence of brutal racism, we all know brokenness and division at some level, whether through divorce, abuse, social injustice, conflict in our community or right inside our own family. We live together in a broken world, and we do not have to live long to learn that we need healing. We need reconciliation. We know from experience that our world is broken and needs to be fixed.

But our problem is even deeper than this. We've also seen enough to know that our attempts to fix the problems of this world further reveal the depths of our brokenness. The worst evils are committed not only in the name of evil but also in crusades in the name of fixing what is broken. Genocide attempts to wipe out whole peoples in order to "cleanse" society of entire ethnic groups. Wars are always waged for the sake of peace. On the interpersonal level, we're always harshest to our friends when we think we need to fix them or feel the need to protect ourselves.

We know the world is broken, and we know we're too broken to fix it ourselves. We teach our children a realist's rhyme: "Humpty Dumpty sat on a wall / Humpty Dumpty had a great fall / And all the kings horses and all the kings men / Couldn't put Humpty Dumpty back together again." But Humpty-Dumpty realism begs the question, can anyone fix us? What or who is out there beyond our landscapes of brokenness?

In the modern world we try to bracket this question even as we seek reconciliation. We are aware that differences in religion can create conflict. So we try to find common ground without reference to anything beyond the common human experience. This makes reconciliation a very popular yet hopelessly vague (and therefore increasingly unhelpful) concept. It also forces some (especially those who have suffered great injustice) to insist that reconciliation is not the right goal in human conflict. "When were we ever unified?" they ask.

Without reference to an explicit beyond, we are left with versions of reconciliation that offer little concrete hope that fundamental change is possible. We want to be clear: when we talk about the "beyond," we mean the God who is revealed in Christian Scripture as Creator and Redeemer of the cosmos, the God of Israel who raised the crucified Jesus from the dead. A Christian vision of reconciliation needs a theological foundation. More than that, however, the term *beyond* reminds us that reconciliation is a journey beyond our own vision, beyond human actors and our strategies and programs. God's desire and vision is beyond our desire and vision. Reconciliation is not merely the sum total of our work; it's also the peculiar gift we learn to receive as we live into the story of God's people. This explicit reference to God's story is missing in the prevailing versions of reconciliation today.

RECONCILIATION AS INCREASINGLY POPULAR

Reconciliation has become a popular notion in our time, finding its way into the political rhetoric and public policy of many governments. South Africa and its apparently successful Truth and Reconciliation Commission have captured the imagination of many post-conflict societies (including Rwanda, Bosnia and some southern cities in the United States) as they debate the merits and possibility of such a commission in their own countries or communities. Interest in reconciliation in the academic world has increased, with scholarship on the topic and with institutions setting up "reconciliation studies" in the growing world of "peace studies" programs. Faith-based and other nongovernmental organizations (NGOs) in conflict areas around the world are working for reconciliation alongside Christian ministries that have adopted reconciliation as one of their goals.

It is perhaps not surprising that reconciliation has become a common goal. The end of the Cold War did not bring in the new world order of peace that many had hoped for. On the contrary, fragmentation, war, violence and civil unrest in a world polarized between rich and poor continue. Ethnic and religious identities seem to intensify as cultural and family ties disintegrate. In the midst of such a fragmented and broken world, reconciliation is a rallying cry for some hope of peace, solidarity and a better world.

With this growing popularity, reconciliation has become a vast buffet line from which anyone from power brokers to minority groups can pick and choose whatever they might want. The result is a fuzziness concerning reconciliation—and with it the danger that reconciliation's popularity may result in it meaning nothing. In an attempt to appeal to as wide a constituency as possible, we leave reconciliation to stand on its own, without reference to an explicit vision of life and society toward which it should lead.

We have been at many reconciliation events where people shed tears and exchanged hugs. But after those events, we always ask, what next? People usually go back to their normal way of life. What and where are the patterns of life and social structures to sustain a vision of reconciliation? Without them, reconciliation devolves into a one-time event. The question we want to ask is, reconciliation *toward what?*

RECONCILIATION AS INDIVIDUAL SALVATION

An emphasis on right relationship with God is crucial to a Christian vision of reconciliation. Faithful obedience to God is an invitation into a whole new way of life, a journey with God where our desires are increasingly transformed toward God's desires.

Yet there is a widespread notion in some of the most energetic contemporary Christian movements that the biblical call to reconciliation is solely about reconciling God and humanity, with no reference to social realities. In this view, preaching, teaching, church life and mission are only about a personal relationship between people and God. Christian energy is focused on winning converts, planting and growing churches, and evangelistic efforts. We have heard pastors say, "We appreciate the work you're doing, but as the leader of my church I'm called to stay focused on the gospel and not get distracted by other ministries." For them, Christianity is exclusively about personal piety and morals.

Another variety of this version of reconciliation is the explosive momentum of preaching and teaching centered on guarantees of personal prosperity. The gospel of wealth sells well in the United States, and it is doing even better in Africa, drawing in people by the thousands. I (Emmanuel) talked to a pastor in Rwanda who told me how enthusiastic he was about the growth of his megachurch outside Kigali. He did not mention his country's recent history of genocide. He was so confident that God was blessing his parishioners that he did not think it important to address the recent history of violence between Christians in his country.

Some have rightly described this as the "gospel of evacuation." This false gospel promises either an afterlife of eternal bliss or blessings for individual well-being, which are not connected to the transformation of social realities. As we have written with a number of other Christian leaders from throughout the world, "the transmission of the gospel and the ministry of the church do not run in a pure, separate historical stream, but are carried on inside of and tainted by the world's poisoned, muddy histories. All the agents of brokenness must be discerned and confronted—personal, social, and spiritual."[1]

The problem with individualistic Christianity is what we call "reconciliation without memory," an approach that ignores the wounds of the world and proclaims peace where there is no peace (see Jer 8:11). This shallow kind of Christianity does not take local places and their history of trauma, division and oppression seriously. It abandons the past too quickly and confidently in search of a new future. Reconciliation as evacuation detaches the gospel from social realities and leaves that messy world to social agencies and governments. The result is a dualistic theology and superficial discipleship that separates individual salvation from social transformation.

RECONCILIATION AS CELEBRATING DIVERSITY

One of the most widespread and cherished notions of our time is that reconciliation is about promoting diversity in a pluralistic world. In a shrinking world of rising conflict over identity and difference, where we all face the presence of more and more ethnic "strangers" in our midst, many seek a common ground on which to unite humanity. Nearly every American university has a center for multiculturalism. Promoting diversity just makes good business sense. Reconciliation becomes synonymous with celebrating difference or with making institutions and societies more "inclusive" of diverse people groups.

One positive contribution of the focus on diversity and multiculturalism has been to acknowledge that differences are not a threat but a gift to our life together. How boring when legitimate social, historical, cultural and ethnic differences are dissolved into a world of drab uniformity, a world without color, where all cats are gray. Even if such a world were possible, no one would want to live in it. The unique particularities of colors, histories, geographies and cultures make life interesting.

The problem arises when each group begins to think it is self-sufficient in its own identity. Moreover, in the absence of an explicit beyond, it is not clear what diversity really means, whose interests it serves, what it leads toward or why it is a good thing. For Christians, the language of reconciliation is not grounded in a historical or sociological reality, but in a theological one. A vision of reconciliation grounded in the story of God not only affirms diversity but also displays it as part of God's purpose in creation. We are created with different gifts for the sake of playing different roles in Christ's body (see 1 Cor 12:12-31). God's story also names how all our diverse loyalties and allegiances have been compromised by Adam and Eve's rebellion against God (see Gen 3). If the world is diverse in ways that should be celebrated, we contend that it is also diverse in ways that are deeply disordered because of long histories of separation, injustice and struggles for power.

That is why a vision of reconciliation limited to "diversity" or "inclusion" does not go far enough. It easily becomes another ground on which interest groups contend for more power, failing to offer a higher vision than promoting one's ethnicity or gender or culture as ends in themselves. Diversity fails to deliver a vision that makes it worth deep personal, cultural and national sacrifices such as being transformed by strangers, engaging enemies and absorbing pain without passing it on. Too often "diversity" becomes a cheap form of coalition building by essentially silencing difference, as in interreligious efforts that presume all religions are basically the same. An authentic way to work together in a pluralistic world is not to silence our differences but to truthfully share the convictions by which we see the world and to seek the common ground where that leads us.

RECONCILIATION AS ADDRESSING INJUSTICE

Another prevailing vision maintains that reconciliation must never be mentioned without saying "justice" in the same breath. Sometimes it is even claimed that justice must precede reconciliation. It is easy to understand the basis of this claim. Often reconciliation has been invoked as a naive, "can't we all get along?" sentimentality or as the agenda of the powerful to "move on" without facing intricate demands for justice.

Much is at stake in who is saying "reconciliation," what they mean by it and the experience and story out of which they speak. "No reconciliation without justice" can be an attempt to resist a politically or historically naïve vision of reconciliation that doesn't take into account the complex processes and long history through which people's sense of who they are has become connected to the past and its conflicts.

Once when I (Chris) was speaking about racial reconciliation to a group of black pastors in Houston, one said, "Look, you can't talk about reconciliation apart from liberation." He went on to talk about the historical politics of public education in Houston. He pointed out how whites and blacks were voting differently on an upcoming school bond issue based on their interests. He said the pursuit of a new relationship must not overlook the realities of power and insisted that these issues needed to be on the table when pursuing a new racial future in Houston.

Talk of reconciliation alone, especially when it sounds like a call to forget the past and move on, threatens not only the future of particular communities but individual identities as well. Martin Luther King Jr. often talked about the need for African-Americans to be integrated *into* power, not out of it. Minority groups feel this in particular. They know intimately the dangers of the false prophets who say, "'Peace, peace' but there is no peace" (Jer 8:11).

For others, seeing justice as prior to reconciliation is connected to beliefs about a deeply fallen world and the political realism associated with such beliefs. Given that all human enterprises are marked by sin, many believe war and conflict are inevitable consequences of this fallen reality. There will always be enemies. Instead of pretending we can build a perfect world where all hostilities are reconciled, we are better off accepting these tragic facts and concentrating our efforts on designing policies and structures that allow us to secure "the greatest good for the greatest number of people." That is what justice promises.

No doubt, a strong emphasis on justice is crucial as it embraces the truth about evil and sin in the world. However, the challenge is, whose justice? The definition of justice is not self-evident. If it is to make sense or to lead to a transformed vision of human relations, justice requires a story. The justice of the Lord's Table, for example, is not simply a punitive or retributive justice but a far more radical form, pursued within a vision of costly communion to bring together what has been torn apart.

Accordingly, if there is the "realism" that notes the limits of living in a sinful world, there is also the "realism" of the transforming, mysterious power that raised Jesus from the dead. Acts of injustice can be punished, repented of, publicly named and denounced, or even repaid, but they can never be undone. No act of justice can make up for the horrific loss of an abducted child or for the trauma of a near-death beating. Within a vision of pure, tit-for-tat, "realistic" justice, forgiveness can look naive indeed.

The quest for reconciliation and the quest for doing justice are closely connected to the quest for truth—not only the truth about "what went wrong" and how that is mended but also the truth about God's costly embrace of an undeserving humanity in spite of all that has gone wrong. Christians are a people whose life is to be a sign and ferment within the world, pointing to the truth about God's grace. One insufficient version of Christian mission is reconciliation without memory, jumping over the past too quickly by offering cheap grace to those who have done wrong and never repented.

But the other extreme is to create sophisticated initiatives that speak of redressing the structural results of historical injustices yet do not cast the vision of a new future of community and friendship between historic enemies. We call this "justice without communion." A future of shared life with enemies requires a long journey of persuasion and transformation of hearts, minds and desires. Such a future may seem unreasonably costly, but Jesus' story is a constant reminder that we live not by the logic of cause and effect but rather by the mysterious order of death and resurrection.

RECONCILIATION AS FIREFIGHTING

In the absence of a clear vision of where it leads, reconciliation has largely become a matter of addressing the urgent needs of division and conflict—relief, mediation, advocacy and conflict resolution. The image that comes to mind is that of firefighting—pragmatically trying to "put out" (or at least minimize) local and national fires of conflict, division, war and brokenness. In firefighting, we always need more water, better equipment and better-trained fighters. The focus is on better techniques. As a result, programs, initiatives and studies of reconciliation focus on developing and delivering skills, processes, strategies and how-to guides to places of conflict. More and more we look to professional "peacebuilders" and "reconcilers" as reconciliation becomes the exclusive terrain of "experts."

We see this in work to decrease violence, feed the hungry, bind up the broken, forge truces in conflict situations and negotiate cooperation between historic enemies. Such works of mercy are desperately needed. Indeed, it is central to the Christian vision to practice and support such works. Many Christians not only engage in these but also lead the way around the world, from the governmental level to the grassroots. Some have even suggested that Christianity provides the deep motivation required for works of mercy, justice, forgiveness and truth-telling in a broken world.

However, in serving these social aspirations, Christianity can become one more way to achieve the same ends as an NGO or state diplomacy. If reconciliation as evacuation disconnects the gospel from social realities, reconciliation as firefighting transforms the church into a social agency. It is often unclear whether what Christians believe and practice makes any difference for what reconciliation looks like. The church fails to offer a unique answer to that crucial question, reconciliation *toward what?*

At best, Christian beliefs are seen as providing motivation to do more and better firefighting, to service the same ends sought by the "real" players in the worlds of diplomacy and statecraft. The church is the ambulance driver while others put out fires. What Christians believe does not seem to offer a unique vision of healing in the midst of conflict or of human flourishing on the ground in real places. It is still the same world of fire, water, hoses, ambulances.

What we need is not simply better gear and techniques but a story that helps us remember another world is possible. The good news is that God's story offers us just that. In the midst of our world's deep brokenness, God's kingdom breaks in to create new possibilities.

In the small French town where the mentally disabled men and the lonely academic lived, a parish priest offered a bit of pastoral guidance to Jean Vanier. Vanier asked the priest what he should do with his life. The priest said, "Invite these two disabled men to live with you." This small act of trust and hospitality birthed the first L'Arche (the Ark) community. Today in some 130 L'Arche communities throughout the world, thousands of people with disabilities and long-term assistants share daily life in family-like homes within neighborhoods and towns. While L'Arche certainly works to help disabled people reach their full potential in society, Vanier maintains that the heart of their vocation is "communion" between the disabled and "temporarily-abled," across their mutual isolation, as they eat together and transform one another in the process.

As John Perkins recovered from the beating that had almost killed him, he had time to think. Lying on that hospital bed, he believed he was done with white people. But God interrupted his thoughts with a vision of an interracial community in the heart of Mississippi. Over the next four decades, defying the refrain that

Sunday is America's most segregated hour, the Voice of Calvary congregation and community development organization Perkins planted maintained a vibrant interracial life across economic boundaries. Inspired by this vision, many others started similar beloved communities in America's inner cities, with thousands joining in a movement called the Christian Community Development Association.

When Billy Neal Moore was in jail, awaiting the trial in which he would be sentenced to death, a minister shared with him the good news that Jesus loved him and wanted to forgive his sins. Moore learned that no one is beyond redemption. From prison, he wrote to his victim's family and asked their forgiveness. Astoundingly, they immediately wrote back to say that they also were Christians and that they forgave him. Then the family decided to petition the Georgia parole board to commute Moore's death sentence. In 1991, Moore was paroled from prison, transformed by the grace of God and his victim's family members. "When I was released, they embraced me like a brother," Moore said of Stapton's family. He has been preaching the gospel of forgiveness to schoolchildren and church groups ever since.[2]

In the painful aftermath of his near-fatal bomb injuries, Michael Lapsley struggled to find the real hope God offers to people who would rather kill their neighbors than have to deal with them. Knowing that the future we imagine has everything to do with how we remember the past, Lapsley founded the Institute for the Healing of Memories in South Africa. At this retreat center, thousands of everyday South Africans of all colors and backgrounds have taken intensive weekend journeys together into healing their wounds of violence and separation. It has become a place where all South Africans can gather to imagine a new future, even as they live in a society unimaginable in 1990.

We can never forget the rest of Angelina Atyam's story. She refused to be silent when her daughter was abducted. Atyam and other mothers of abducted children began the Concerned Parents' Association, seeking the release of the children while advocating a different approach toward their captors. "Our message is unconditional forgiveness and reconciliation," she said. "We have absolutely forgiven them. We can turn to a fresh page; we do it for the sake of the children who are alive." She continued, "I have waited more than three years; some parents even longer. We are tired of war, and our children need a better life. Of revenge I would say that we cannot throw petrol on a burning fire; otherwise we would be like them. We can say this because we have been at the center of the pain."[3]

At the center of pain, God breaks in to reveal a new creation. Within landscapes of deep brokenness, these five interrupted lives were sustained by particular convictions about God and God's mission of reconciliation in a broken world. Apart from these convictions, their journeys do not make sense in a world where the endless cycle of "an eye for an eye" and group self-interest is the norm. These five journeys embody a unique vision of reconciliation, somehow received from beyond the normal realm of human actors.

This book is about unveiling God's distinct vision of reconciling all things in Jesus Christ. The prevailing visions of reconciliation in our church and society are insufficient because they cannot make sense of stories like those of Jean Vanier, John Perkins, Billy Neal Moore, Michael Lapsley and Angelina Atyam. We need a new vision for reconciliation, and we believe God has provided it in the peculiar story of Scripture. But we don't just believe it because it sounds good or because we're unsatisfied with the other options. We believe it because we've seen it in the lives of people and communities transformed by the ministry of reconciliation, and we have experienced it in our own journeys. We believe it because we've been caught up in the story of God that continues to unfold in the midst of our broken world.

So we'd like to invite you to step back from the world of prevailing visions and rediscover this story with us. Maybe you can even catch a glimpse of what God's new world might look like in the midst of the brokenness you know intimately. We want to begin by remembering together the story of God's new creation.

2

Stepping Back

Reconciliation as the Goal of God's Story

*T*he brokenness of our world is as personal as a divided marriage or family, as hidden as the shared loneliness of the affluent and the disabled, and as large as long-divided people groups in places like Mississippi, South Africa, Rwanda and Northern Ireland. But emptied of a vision bigger than us and our interests, reconciliation in such landscapes is diluted into a popular and vague precept, synonymous with individual salvation, merely a celebration of diversity, a method for addressing injustice or a way to put out fires of conflict.

In spite of the problems these various visions have created for reconciliation, we cannot shy away from the language of reconciliation. Christians believe that reconciliation is a gift from God. It is God's language for a broken world. Rather than retreat from this language, we are challenged by the shortcomings of these prevailing visions to articulate a fresh account of why Christians should care about reconciliation—an account that is grounded in a vision of the beyond and also confronts the real brokenness of the world.

THE NEED TO STEP BACK

To appreciate why Christians should care about reconciliation, we need to step back from the dominant expectations that reconciliation has to do either with personal salvation alone or with mediation and conflict resolution (hence the dominant images of reconciliation as either escapist evacuation or emergency firefighting). Given the many forms of brokenness in the world, we sense an urgent need to either hide ourselves from the social realities or to act. So our call to step back might easily be misunderstood as another escapist recommendation. Recently, as we talked about the vision and shape of Christian reconciliation in the world, a colleague gently reminded us, "The fire is out there raging. What we need is water to put it out, not empty and distracting theological discussions."

But stepping back from the dominant firefighting approach is neither irrelevant nor inappropriate. Quite the opposite. For Christians, the ability to step back from how we see and act in the world is a crucial dimension of practicing our faith. This is exactly because we believe that the world did not begin with us but with God. Simply put, Christians contend there is a world beyond the world of fires. We return to our insistence on the need for a beyond. If Christians are to reconnect the world of fires and firefighting to the story of God, stepping back is crucial. Such a connection not only rightly inspires Christian commitment toward firefighting, it reshapes and informs our patterns of living in the world.

As Salvadoran Archbishop Oscar Romero said, "It helps, now and then, to step back and take the long view. The kingdom is not only beyond our efforts, it is even beyond our vision. . . . We are workers, not master builders; ministers, not messiahs. We are prophets of a future not our own."[1] It is the very ability to step back that allows Christians to see rightly what is going on in the world and to imagine new possibilities for living out a vision that comes from beyond the world of fires. Thus the ability to step back is not inaction but an invitation into a different kind of action—a different way of seeing and thus engaging the world around us.

Stepping back, therefore, is not a retreat from the world of brokenness but an invitation to receive God's imagination for the world. Because Christians believe that the world with all its mess is still the province of God's reign and ongoing redemption, stepping back is a way of connecting the brokenness of the world to the story of God and discovering the many gifts that story offers to help us understand reconciliation. As Moses said to Israel at the Red Sea, "The LORD will fight for you; you need only to be still" (Ex 14:14 NIV). Stillness, then, is a posture not only of learning to see what is going on in the world but of learning to trust God and God's vision for our redemption. This is what makes the ability to step back from a focus on skills, resources and strategies so critical in any attempt to rediscover a Christian vision and practice of reconciliation.

WHAT IS CHRISTIAN ABOUT RECONCILIATION?

Our conviction is this: while never neglecting works of mercy and justice in a broken world, theology matters. A Christian vision of reconciliation cannot be conceived or sustained without the particular life of the God whom Christians confess, the living God of Israel who raised the crucified Jesus from the dead. The life and preaching of Jesus shape our lives distinctly in a broken world.

Shaped by convictions about God, our faith and practice point us to a deeper vocation of hope, offering a vision of what the journey of reconciliation looks like in this world, where that journey leads, how people who enter that journey are transformed along the way and how that journey relates to neighbors, strangers and enemies. Christianity does not exist to motivate people for work within the prevailing visions of reconciliation. Rather, Christianity offers distinct gifts of seeing, speaking about, engaging and being transformed within the world and its brokenness.

While this vision has often been implicit, we contend it must be made explicit. Without a clear theological vision, God's dream of reconciliation offers no better hope to a world that groans for another way. Without being explicitly articulated, the vision cannot be sustained. It is inevitably replaced by dominant social visions. And the church begins to look and sound like one more social agency or NGO, or an escapist flight from social pain.

We are claiming that there is a deeper, richer hope God offers to the world. Yet we have forgotten the very source that makes reconciliation a distinct gift and vision of hope. When we step back, two things come clear: first, God's life-giving vision grows out of a story; and second, that story is about a quieter revolution.

THE STORY

The life-giving connection and the gifts that flow from a deeper hope cannot be seized from just anywhere. They are connected to and received from a story.

In summary, that story goes like this: "So if anyone is in Christ, there is a new creation: everything old has passed away; see, everything has become new! All this is from God, who reconciled us to himself through Christ, and has given us the ministry of reconciliation" (2 Cor 5:17-18 NRSV). There are two movements in this story, and the order is important. The first movement is about God and what God has done in Christ. The second is about the transformation this first movement has enacted in the world and in the lives of people.

Already we see that one way of misreading this story about reconciliation is to immediately bring ourselves into the picture. In our action-infected world, we are tempted to first ask what we must do, jumping into action without dwelling on the gift God gives. But the story of 2 Corinthians 5 reminds us that before reconciliation is about us, it is about God. It is God's mission in the world. The journey of reconciliation begins with seeing that reconciliation is not the goal of human striving but is instead a gift God longs for us to accept. It is connected with and gives birth to other gifts within the reality of God's new creation.

Another way of misreading the story is to see reconciliation as solely a vertical movement, restoring people to God. That restoration is certainly at the heart of the story and its good news. But what is also clear from this story is that many other gifts flow from God's gift of reconciliation, including a special commission. Paul continues: "We are therefore Christ's ambassadors, as though God were making his appeal through us. We implore you on Christ's behalf: Be reconciled to God" (v. 20 NIV). Within the reality of "reconciling the world to himself in Christ" (v. 19 NIV), God's gift of reconciliation disrupts neat distinctions between vertical and horizontal. This story is about both the interior and the exterior, contemplation and action, sanctuary and streets, heart and body, worship and activism, theory and practice, desires and deeds, preaching and living, individual and community, baptism and politics, praying and prophesying, church and world.

God's mission of reconciliation challenges, moves beyond, even explodes these conventional distinctions.

A QUIETER REVOLUTION

Stepping back and connecting reconciliation to God's story also helps us move away from dramatic visions of fixing the world, as if our job were to provide solutions to problems outside us. If Christians believe anything, it is that no one—including ourselves and the church—is separate from the brokenness as an untainted solution to the problems of our world. The new creation contends with the old. The dividing line between good and evil runs straight through each one of us. So the journey of reconciliation begins with a transformation of the human person.

The stories of Scripture point to reconciliation as a costly journey of transformation and hope that includes (but goes far deeper than) firefighting—a quiet revolution that takes shape over time and bursts forth through signs of hope in local places. Grounded in God's gift of the new creation, a Christian vision insists that reconciliation is ultimately about the transformation of the everyday—a quiet revolution that occurs over time in everyday people, everyday congregations, everyday communities, amid the most broken places on God's earth.

When I (Chris) first came to Jackson, Mississippi, I thought I had arrived to solve racism and poverty. I'd come to spend a little time fixing Mississippi white folks and fixing the poor, and then I planned to go on with a career in national government, where I thought the real action was. But the people at Voice of Calvary taught me about a "quiet revolution." Part of this long, revolutionary process was my own conversion from my deep desire to be a "fixer" to seeing my need to be changed by people radically different from me— including many of the very people I had come to fix. Grounded in God's gift of a new creation, a Christian vision insists that reconciliation is ultimately about this transformation of the everyday.

By stepping back, we're able to see that God is always planting seeds of hope—but not in the ways we might have anticipated or chosen. We must gain the eyes to see this hope because this quiet revolution often happens under the radar screen. The task of recovering reconciliation as a Christian vision is also a recovery of real, overlooked stories in history. It means learning to listen to people who embody a unique journey and set of practices in a broken and divided world.

Even when the work of places like Perkins's Voice of Calvary or Atyam's Concerned Parents' Association is acknowledged, we rarely notice how the continuity of such work depends on an evangelical root. Such communities of reconciliation are not possible without transformative experiences and engagements sustained by prayer and listening to God, life together as worshiping communities, a sense of belonging to places of pain, the long-term power of persuasion, and practices such as the capacity to absorb pain without passing that pain on to others. All of these arise from deep convictions about God and Jesus Christ.

We begin by attending to the story of God. We remember it in worship. We tell it to our children. We memorize its most poignant phrases and ask where God wants to speak them again through us. With Ruth from the Bible and Jean Vanier of L'Arche we say, "Where you go, I will go, and where you stay I will stay. Your people will be my people and your God my God" (Ruth 1:16 NIV). With Jesus and John Perkins we learn to say, "Father, forgive them, for they do not know what they are doing" (Lk 23:34 NIV). Because a Christian vision of reconciliation is rooted in the story of God's people, we can grasp the vision only as we learn to inhabit the story. The story shapes us in the habits of God's peculiar people; the more we get it down inside us, the easier it is to resist the temptations of this world's prevailing visions.

3

Reconciliation
Is a Journey with God

$\mathcal{O}$ne of the core convictions that drove the civil rights movement in the United States was the exhortation "God can make a way out of no way!" It is important to realize that this affirmation from the black church came out of a long history of reading Scripture. In the brush arbors of plantations in the American South, slaves gathered to remember the story of God calling Israel out of bondage in Egypt. "God can make a way out of no way," they said, even when it looked like their own slavery would never end. After the Emancipation Proclamation in 1863, black Christians in America continued generation after generation to gather for "watch night" services on New Year's Eve to remember how "God can make a way out of no way!" Remembering God's faithfulness in the past, they shaped a vision for a new society in America—a vision that everyone had to take seriously in the 1960s.

A closer look at the passage of Scripture illuminated in the previous chapter reveals the gifts the biblical story offers for those engaged in the ministry of reconciliation. This crucial passage is in Paul's second letter to the church at Corinth:

> Therefore, if anyone is in Christ, he is a new creation; the old has gone, the new has come! All this is from God, who reconciled us to himself through Christ and gave us the ministry of reconciliation: that God was reconciling the world to himself in Christ, not counting men's sins against them. And he has committed to us the message of reconciliation. We are therefore Christ's ambassadors, as though God were making his appeal through us. (2 Cor 5:17-20 NIV)

The quest for reconciliation in the world is a journey with God. In this passage, Paul highlights a number of marks that distinguish this way of walking in the world from other paths we might choose to take. The content of a Christian vision for reconciliation is made clearer as we pay attention to the image of a journey and the distinctive marks that 2 Corinthians names.

RECONCILIATION IS A JOURNEY

Since "new creation" is the short form of the story Paul is telling, this suggests that to understand the "new" that Christ has ushered in, we have to know something of the original story of creation and the old order that is passing away. This has a number of significant implications.

Even for God, reconciliation is not an event or an achievement, but a journey from "old" to "new." As Scripture recounts the specific shape of this journey, God is not inviting us simply to affirm a list of abstract beliefs but rather to set out on an adventure. If this journey calls for great skillfulness and discipline, the most vital skill required is memory. When Christians remember well, we are able to explore the story of God's involvement with the world and to draw on that story to locate and understand what is going on at any particular time within that story. This is what makes Scripture indispensable to the Christian journey of reconciliation. Scripture both forms Christian memory and shapes concrete possibilities for life in the world. The more Christians are able to ground reconciliation as a journey with God from old toward new, the more we are able to recover the indispensable gifts that sustain that journey and make it possible.

THE CENTER OF THE JOURNEY IS JESUS

In the drama of reconciliation, Jesus is constantly named as the most important person in the story: "If anyone is in *Christ*"; "God who reconciled us to himself in *Christ*"; "We are therefore *Christ's* ambassadors" (2 Cor 5:17-20 NIV). There is no way to overstate either the significance or the scandal of this claim.

During our visit to a class at a prominent peacebuilding program, a couple of students from Ireland led the group in a delightful celebration of St. Patrick's Day. One student directed us in reciting Patrick's famous prayer: "God with me, God before me, God behind me, God in me, God beneath me." But something didn't feel right about the prayer. Later we realized why. To make the words more palatable to non-Christians in the room, the student had replaced the "Christ" of Patrick's prayer with the more generic "God."

The life of St. Patrick, a pursuer of costly peace, could make no sense apart from friendship with and prayer to a very particular person. As will become clearer throughout this book, the journey of reconciliation hangs or falls on seeing Jesus. We must learn to see how the very particularities of his life, death and resurrection are to shape the contours of our own journey. For Christians, the compass for the journey of reconciliation is always pointing toward Jesus Christ.

THE JOURNEY IS NOT FOR EXPERTS ONLY

Another critical mark of the journey illuminated in 2 Corinthians 5 is that reconciliation is not limited to a few but is for "anyone in Christ." Reconciliation is a ministry offered to the world through everyone who has been baptized into Christ's body. It is not just for professionals or pastors or NGO leaders. Reconciliation is the ministry of high-school students, moms, retirees and prison inmates. Indeed, people who do not work as religious or service professionals are often in a better position to join the quiet revolution of God's kingdom. Not captivated by the temptation to do great things for God, they patiently go about the hard work of loving their friends and enemies.

Though widely recognized for his courageous leadership in reconciliation efforts between Jews, Muslims and Christians in the Holy Land, Archbishop Elias Chacour is not very impressed by his own accomplishments. "The real secret to reconciliation," he says, "is that Jewish mothers and Muslim mothers care about their kids. When we had a summer camp and a thousand kids came, we didn't know how we would feed them. But Jewish, Muslim and Christian mothers worked together all day to feed the kids."[1] With pots and pans in hand, they did the real work of reconciliation.

When we jump too quickly to the task, we tend to view reconciliation in terms of a specific ministry, one optional spoke on a wheel to be engaged either by those who are trained in it (experts and professionals) or by those who have the temperament or spiritual gift for it. Yet what 2 Corinthians confirms is that the gift of reconciliation is given to "anyone in Christ"—another way of saying *all* who are in Christ. For Paul this is the good news, the heart of the gospel: "in Christ" we have all become part of God's new creation.

WE ARE CALLED TO BE AMBASSADORS IN THIS JOURNEY

In light of all that God has done, Paul writes, "we are therefore Christ's ambassadors, as though God were making his appeal through us" (2 Cor 5:20 NIV). An ambassador is a representative who bears someone else's message in their absence. Ambassadors live in foreign countries, which they never really call home. Living within a country other than their own, their practices, loyalties, national interests and even their accent appear strange to the citizens of those countries where they are posted. So it is with Christ's ambassadors of reconciliation inside the world's brokenness.

In 2006 we organized a gathering in Uganda of forty African Christian leaders pursuing peace in Uganda and the surrounding countries of Rwanda, southern Sudan, eastern Congo and Burundi. One of our biggest surprises was learning of the incredible courage it took for those leaders to gather. On our final evening together, Congolese United Methodist Bishop Ntambo Nkulu Ntanda spoke of the wars between the countries of the Christians gathered. He told how the old stories about Uganda's former dictator Idi Amin haunted him, how Uganda's recent war with the Congo had taxed him, how he'd never come to Uganda before and was terrified when he arrived at the airport.

But the gathering changed that. "Here Emmanuel, a Ugandan, embraced me when I walked in," Ntanda said. "I had never worshiped with someone from Sudan, and here there is a Sudanese. Here there have been Anglicans, Methodists, Baptists, Catholics and Pentecostals, all worshiping." With a laugh he declared he was extending his stay in Uganda for two days. "If reconciliation happens, they will say it started here. I am going back to the Congo with a new story to tell about Uganda."

Ntanda's story points to our vocation as Christ's ambassadors of reconciliation—a transformation into a new story that resists narrow boundaries and loyalties. In a world turned upside down, we worship One who walked right side up. As we worship and follow Jesus, we are conformed to his strange image. So we bear the strange marks of God's new creation in the midst of a world still in the grip of the old.

Ntanda's story also helps us see that our vocation as Christ's ambassadors involves, or better still *is,* a corporate expression and a form of politics. We are used to thinking of politics as something a government does. Politics is much more, however. It concerns the loyalties and allegiances that shape our whole life, including the public life of the church.

Like ambassadors who work within the dissimilar political realities of their host countries while representing another nation, Christian ministers of reconciliation engage the world's realities while pointing to the reality of a new creation. When many Christians were swept up in the politics of Nazi Germany, for example, and ignored the plight of their Jewish neighbors, the Confessing Church embodied a different loyalty. In the Barmen Declaration they proclaimed at great cost, "We reject the false doctrine, as though there were areas of our life in which we would not belong to Jesus Christ, but to other lords."[2]

God's gift of a call to be Christ's ambassadors of reconciliation intends to unseat other lords—power, nationalism, race or ethnic loyalty as an end in itself—and give birth to deeper allegiances, stories, spaces and communities that are a "demonstration plot" of the reality of God's new creation in Christ. Put simply, reconciliation both names the church as and requires the church to be the sign and agent of God's reconciliation.

WE WALK THE JOURNEY AS JARS OF CLAY

Lest the language of ambassadorship sound grandiose and conjure images of diplomatic immunity and self-importance, Paul reminds us in a passage just before 2 Corinthians 5:17-21 that the gift of reconciliation we have received is a fragile one that involves suffering on our part. He writes:

> But we have this treasure in jars of clay to show that this all-surpassing power is from God and not from us. We are hard pressed on every side, but not crushed; perplexed, but not in despair; persecuted, but not abandoned; struck down, but not destroyed. We always carry around in our body the death of Jesus, so that the life of Jesus may also be revealed in our body. For we who are alive are always being given over to death for Jesus' sake, so that his life may be revealed in our body. (2 Cor 4:7-11 NIV)

That we carry the treasure in jars of clay is an invitation for the Christian to see reconciliation not only as a gift but as a very precious treasure—far more precious than anything we deserve. It is also an invitation to walk tenderly with the treasure, lest we drop it. That is why a key mark of reconciliation is gentleness.

But Paul does not shy away from the challenges of this gift that we have been given. He warns us that, since we are marked by the death of Christ, we *always* carry around the marks of Christ's wounds and death. The Christian journey of reconciliation is a personal journey in which our lives are at stake. Reconciliation is not simply a precious gift; it is a long, hard and costly journey, a journey during which we are constantly pressed on every side, perplexed, persecuted, struck down.

For ten years I (Chris) led a national reconciliation ministry with my friend Spencer Perkins. In 1998 we organized the College, Ethnicity and Reconciliation conference for three hundred leaders working on college campuses across America. The first night of this conference, a group of staff members from Inter-Varsity met and talked about the growing popularity of reconciliation initiatives across the country. They reminded one another and us that this ministry was not a romantic bandwagon to jump on, telling stories of the many people within InterVarsity who had labored on the frontlines of racial challenges and died early deaths. This was work, they said, in which we learn to lay down our lives for the sake of a deeper hope breaking into the world.

The next day, Spencer collapsed in the middle of our meeting and was rushed to the hospital. That night he returned to the meeting, and we gave the final conference talk together. We spoke of "going the long haul," about the struggle in our own relationship over the weeks leading up to the conference and about the power of God's grace, which had given us the resources to forgive one another and to meet the challenge of racial reconciliation in a new way.

That was the last time we spoke together. Three days later, Spencer died from a massive heart attack. For all of us, Spencer's death sealed the truth of both the pain of this struggle and, in the mystery of God's presence in those months of healing and grace, the promise of God to be with us in the darkest hours of our journeys.

This is why Paul's message in 2 Corinthians is not simply a warning about the journey ahead but is also an encouragement. For he notes, "We are hard pressed on every side, but not crushed; perplexed, but not in despair; persecuted, but not abandoned; struck down, but not destroyed . . . therefore we do not lose heart" (2 Cor 4:8-9, 16 NIV). I almost lost my will to go on when Spencer and I were deeply divided. I certainly did not know how I would press on with this call after Spencer's death. But each time, in the two times of greatest pain in my life, God provided gifts of Scripture, the patient love of friends who told me what I needed to hear and offered wisdom I did not have, the grace I did not deserve and the prayer that gave me strength to simply take the next step. In the mystery of God's presence, all of this somehow enabled me to go on in spite of the "now" and to see new life emerge in ways I could never have imagined.

We're able to not lose heart because we look beyond the now, beyond the visible, and remember the story of God. Without that story, we would be overwhelmed, crushed, destroyed. That is why stepping back from relentless activism is essential in order to "fix our eyes not on what is seen, but on what is unseen. For what is seen is temporary, but what is unseen is eternal" (v. 18). Paul knows that we need not lose heart, because once we fix our gaze on Jesus, we see that he not only invites us to follow a distinctive way in the world; he also offers gifts for the journey. It's to these gifts that we now turn.

4

How Scripture Reshapes Us

*T*he vision of reconciliation as a journey stands in stark contrast to seeing reconciliation primarily as an achievement, an event, a strategy or a program. Furthermore, to see reconciliation as a journey *with God* is to let go of control. This makes it possible for us to receive the good and distinctive gifts God gives to inspire and sustain our journey in the real places of a broken world. As we move deeper into the biblical story, we receive gifts to help us find our way. One of these gifts is Scripture itself. If the church is to sustain a Christian vision and practice of reconciliation, we must become a people reshaped by the Bible.

PEACE AND HARMONY AS GOD'S GIFT TO THE WORLD
Scripture is central to the journey of reconciliation because it relocates us "in the beginning," giving us not just a sense of how everything started but also the chance to rediscover peace and

harmony as God's original gift to creation. Reading the creation account of Genesis 1:1-31, we see God at work creating not just living creatures but peace, order and harmony from the chaos of a formless void. At various stages in this process, God looks at the emerging order of God's work and declares it "good."

The Bible's first account of creation makes clear that not until the sixth day are man and woman created. Even though they are told to "fill the earth and subdue it" (v. 28 NIV), this too is a gift from God: "God blessed them and said . . . " This is why it is dangerous to think of human beings as co-creators with God. We were not there in the beginning. We were not there when God created the birds of the air and the fish of the sea. And while we are called to be peacemakers, we are not the ones who ultimately create peace and order. Scripture reminds us that our call to make peace is preceded by God's gift of a peaceful creation.

TIME TO CULTIVATE THE HABITS OF PEACE

The "in the beginning" story also helps us to remember that God not only creates peace and harmony out of chaos but also takes six days to complete the work of creation. God does not choose to create with a snap of the finger. For some reason, God takes time. Or, to put it differently, creation takes God time.

This biblical vision is important in sustaining our patience in the pursuit of peace and reconciliation. We know that the gift of reconciliation takes time to unfold. But the creation story helps us to see that time itself is God's gift to the world. In other words, we must give ourselves and others time and space to become new people. The work of God's reconciliation is not just about the momentous occasions of bringing Palestinians and Israelis to the negotiating table. It includes taking time to cultivate the habits of ordinary peaceful existence—habits like listening, welcoming strangers, planting gardens, raising children and keeping house.

As the prophet Jeremiah told God's people in exile, we are to seek the peace of the places where we find ourselves.

> Build houses and settle down; plant gardens and eat what they produce. Marry and have sons and daughters; find wives for your sons and give your daughters in marriage, so that they too may have sons and daughters. . . . Seek the peace and prosperity of the city to which I have carried you into exile. Pray to the LORD for it, because if it prospers, you too will prosper. (Jer 29:5-7, NIV)

When we take time to cultivate both the land beneath our feet and the habits that make for healthy existence, we are actively receiving the gift of God's peace.

In a recovery community called New Jerusalem Now in inner-city Philadelphia, addicts help one another heal and actively engage the society that made them sick. Margaret McKenna, a Medical Missions sister, founded the community and is revered as a spiritual mother to scores of people whose lives have been transformed by the power of God in that place. Sister Margaret is a tireless worker whose accomplishments could fill a book twice the size of this one. But every spring in a neighborhood that has suffered church flight and urban blight, she plants a garden. It's a beautiful garden, full of hearty vegetables and colorful flowers. She takes time to weed and water it during the week, and she takes time to enjoy its beauty while celebrating sabbath. Some years back, the *Philadelphia Inquirer* caught wind of Sister Margaret's garden patch and named it "Garden of the Year." We can't help but think that the newspaper's designation was more profound than their award committee knew.

REST IN A BROKEN AND CONSTANTLY BUSY WORLD

In the Genesis creation story, the work of creation is finished by God on the sixth day. Then, on the seventh day, God rests. This account can help us to see that in the midst of the chaos and conflict around us, we are invited to rest. Because God rests, we too can live in restful sabbath with the assurance that the gift of peace is God's to give—and that God can give it without our help. This is not an invitation to become unconcerned about the conflict and chaos in the world but to imagine that the salvation of the world does not ultimately depend on us. God wants to teach us how to rest even as we work for peace and harmony in the world, secure in the knowledge that God loves us and is able to give us the rest we need.

In the movie *Hotel Rwanda,* Paul Rusesabagina is the manager of an elite hotel in Kigali at the height of the 1994 genocide in Rwanda. The movie tells the story of Paul's heroic effort to save hundreds of Tutsis by offering them refuge at the hotel. At one point in the movie, United Nations troops have just been pulled out of Kigali, and the hotel has run out of water and food. The militias that have been slaughtering Tutsis for days encamp in the hotel compound, waiting for orders to attack the people hiding in the hotel.

Fear and panic are everywhere. It is up to Paul, as the hotel manager, to calm everyone and to negotiate with the head of the militia forces. He is exhausted and realizes that the end may be near. But, in a wonderfully moving scene, he takes his wife to the hotel's roof and in the midst of the mayhem opens a bottle of champagne, lights candles and enjoys with her what might be their last time together.

We submit that sabbath in a broken world is something like that—knowing in the midst of action when it is time to be still on a rooftop, even as the whole world is falling apart, spending time with the God we love. When the One we love whispers to us, "All will be well," it is more than wishful thinking. It is the fundamental truth of the universe. All will be well indeed, because the One who created all things does not rest just to take a break. God rests to take a seat on the throne of all creation's praise. Sabbath is the time when we remember that we are in the hands of the God who rules the universe with love.

THE GIFT OF ANOTHER WAY TO PEACE

We also discover from the "in the beginning" story that if peace and harmony are gifts from God, conflict, violence and war are the result of our attempts to grab (and thus secure for ourselves) what we can receive only as a gift from God. The second creation account in Genesis 2 develops even more explicitly the theme we noted in relation to the first account—namely, that all is a gift. God gives Adam and Eve life. God plants a garden for them. God brings all creatures to them to name as they please. God gives them everything they need, and then he adds a commandment, which on the surface appears rather strange: "From any tree of the garden you may eat freely; but from the tree of the knowledge of good and evil you shall not eat" (Gen 2:16-17).

God is telling Adam and Eve, "I will give you everything you need. You can only receive it. You can never take it." But this is exactly what Adam and Eve attempt to do. In the story of the Fall, which immediately follows (see Gen 3), Adam and Eve grab, seize and take hold of the only thing God has not given to them. When we live by a posture of seizing and grabbing in an attempt to be in control of our destinies, we lose the gifts of harmony and peace. The effects of such action are depicted in the rest of the story of Genesis 3: social disruption, enmity, loss of paradise, death.

The history behind the 1994 Rwandan genocide is telling in this regard. The Belgian colonial authorities in Rwanda gave power to minority Tutsis, saying that they were racially superior to the majority Hutus. This order shaped Rwandan life for the first half of the twentieth century. But when Rwanda gained its independence from Belgium, the majority Hutus seized power, pointing to the injustice that had been committed against them for generations. Though Rwanda was a deeply "Christian" nation, neither Hutus nor Tutsis questioned the racial identities assigned to them by colonial authorities. Grasping for power, they forgot the identity they shared as Christians and the new creation that God has made possible in their midst. In 1994 the tensions created by their racial identities exploded into genocide.

There are certainly many sociological, economic, political, anthropological and historical attempts to explain conflict in the world. Many of these accounts help us to understand the truth about our world. But they do not address our deepest problem unless they are able to point to this "original sin," which is the attempt to secure for ourselves what can be received only as a gift. The Christian practice of reconciliation has to do with recovering a posture of receptivity and gratitude as a key virtue—the original virtue—for Christian living in a divided world.

THE DRAMA INSIDE GOD'S STORY

Fortunately, the story of creation does not end with the Fall but continues with God's promise of restoration. It is important, however, to let the first three chapters of Scripture set the tone for what is at stake in the rest of the story. In other words, recovering reconciliation as God's story is an invitation to approach Scripture with a sense of adventure. We learn to live the question, what happens next? Scripture is neither a catalogue of spiritual insights nor a collection of moral guidelines and principles. It is a story. As a story, Scripture can be read through the central plot of Creation, Fall, Promise and Restoration—a plot that is in essence the movement from old creation to new creation.

When we read the story this way, the various episodes, events and promises of Scripture take on new meaning as moments in the journey. Whether it is God's call to Abraham, the various journeys of the patriarchs, the delivery from Egypt, the covenant at Mount Sinai, exile into Babylon, the trek of Joseph and Mary to Bethlehem, the climb of Mary's son to Golgotha or Peter running to the empty tomb, in every case Scripture invites us to see the shape that the journey to new creation takes in the history of a particular people.

Yet throughout the journey of Scripture, the same drama of the first three chapters of Genesis plays over and over again. We encounter a God who continues to give us what we need to live in peace, teaching Israel a way of life in the wilderness. We see our human desire to secure without God what we need, even as God's people tried to take the Promised Land by their own strength, and failed. And we see God's promise of renewal and restoration, as when Israel is able to cross over the Jordan after forty years in the wilderness. The story of Scripture hangs on this theme of movement toward new creation.

Lest we miss this point, God gives out constant reminders, like this one in Isaiah 65:17: "For behold, I create new heavens and a new earth." And to the extent that the story of Scripture ends, it ends with the gift of this new creation finally coming down from heaven, with John declaring, "Then I saw a new heaven and a new earth . . . coming down out of heaven from God, prepared as a bride" (Rev 21:1-2 NRSV).

A CLOUD OF WITNESSES TO INSPIRE US

The new heaven and new earth is the final vision, the end toward which the journey of reconciliation leads. On the journey we can catch only glimpses of this end, but the hope of a new heaven and a new earth is what sustains us on the journey. Yet it is crucial that Scripture offers not only a description of where we're going but also the gift of concrete examples of others who have made this journey before us. We need examples of people who traveled well—saints whose lives were fundamentally reshaped in light of their anticipation of "things not yet seen."

The letter to the Hebrews describes the lives of Abraham, Sarah, Moses and many other people who lived by faith (see Heb 11). In describing their lives and stories, Scripture inserts us into the company of this "cloud of witnesses" and thus invites us to live, like them, in the present already transformed by the "things not yet seen."

To accept this invitation is to live by the same madness that characterized the lives of these witnesses. We say "madness" because, instead of predicting a future based on the present (the rational thing to do), these individuals reshaped the present according to a vision of the future. This is the madness that the letter to the Hebrews speaks about in the life of Noah, who built an ark when there was no storm; of Abraham, who set out on a journey without a clue about where he was going; of Sarah, ninety years old, who believed that she could have a child; of Moses, who imagined he could confront Pharaoh and his might.

But it is not only biblical "heroes" who live by the madness of things not yet seen. The entire community is invited to live this way. Indeed, their stories are told in Scripture as a reminder and an encouragement of the faith that "anyone in Christ" is called to live. Through stories like these, Scripture keeps alive for all of us the hope of the promises not yet fulfilled. This cloud of witnesses includes all of us and, even more, those who will learn the good news of God's love because of our witness in the world.

Ultimately, we are not called to be heroes, but saints. We do not become exceptional by virtue of our own character. Rather, we have been caught up into the cloud of God's grace. We have become living members of the body of Christ in the world. We know that "anyone in Christ" can live God's new reality now.

THE CAPACITY TO IMAGINE NEW POSSIBILITIES AND ALTERNATIVES

Reading Scripture and dwelling within its distinctive vision shapes new possibilities in our response to the conflicts and brokenness in the world. Quite often the brute realities of the world intimidate and overwhelm us. According to the world's logic, it takes power, strength, money and influence to effect change. And so, given the widespread realities of war, conflict and violence in the world, we feel terribly over-powered and helpless, as if we lack the necessary resources to make any difference.

We feel like David standing in front of Goliath (see 1 Sam 17). But this is precisely why Scripture gives us such a story—to show that there are alternatives and that this task of reconciliation is about imagining new ways to draw from the story of promises not yet fulfilled.

According to the story, Israel is completely overmatched by the Philistines. The champion of the Philistines is the giant Goliath. He walks into battle clothed with a bronze helmet, breast armor and an iron spear. As soon as the Israelites see him, they are understandably terrified. They have two options: either surrender immediately or respond to Goliath's challenge on his terms by picking one of their own, dressing him in armor and standing him in front of Goliath. They know they don't have anyone in their camp who could defeat Goliath on his terms. So they send a young, unexperienced boy named David, with no armor and no weapons except a sling and a bag of smooth stones.

David cuts such a pathetic figure that Goliath is insulted. "Am I a dog, that you come to me with sticks?" Goliath says to David. "Come to me, and I will give your flesh to the birds of the sky and the beasts of the field" (vv. 43-44). The rest of the story is well known. Putting his hand in his bag, David takes out a stone, slings it and strikes the Philistine on the forehead. On that day, little Israel and young David defeat the mighty Philistines.

What can we learn from such a violent story about reconciliation and peacebuilding? For one, it teaches us that when we respond to the challenges of the world with the expected weapons and normal ways of fighting back, we always find ourselves helplessly overmatched. The Christian ministry of reconciliation is about learning to identify, care for and smooth the unique pebbles God provides for us as we confront the Goliaths of this world. When we read David's story alongside the story of Jesus, we begin to see the pebbles God has made available. However weak it may seem to us, we are called to work on skills of forgiveness, self-giving service and costly love of the enemy.

This is what I (Chris) witnessed every day in the life of Spencer Perkins. Here was a man who suffered deep humiliations at the hands of white people—from integrating his public high school and having no one sit next to him for two years, to seeing his bloody father the morning after he was beaten by white police officers. Here was a man who suffered at the hands of black people in the neighborhood. JoJo stole Spencer's car and spread lies about him in the church. But whenever JoJo stopped by the office, I would marvel at Spencer taking the time to listen, to laugh, to tell JoJo what he needed to hear with a mix of truth and humor I had never seen before or since. From outlaws to rednecks, Spencer embraced his enemies on the small ground of West Jackson.

David's audacity to imagine that he could confront Goliath with just a bag of stones also came from his firm conviction that "the LORD does not deliver by sword or by spear, for the battle is the LORD's" (1 Sam 17:47). Unless a Christian pursuit of peace and reconciliation constantly points to this story of "the battle is the LORD's," it can never be sustained. For without this story, Christians lose the resources to cultivate the necessary imagination that shapes Christian alternatives in a world of destructive conflict. In other words, the story of God not only gives Christians motivation to work for reconciliation and peace in the world, it also reshapes the way the challenge is understood and provides concrete alternatives to our usual versions of reconciliation.

THE GIFT OF COMMUNION BEYOND COEXISTENCE

In a conversation we led on race and reconciliation in America, one participant raised an objection: "What are we being reconciled into? Black and white have never been one in the first place. Rather than talk about reconciliation, we should be talking about unity. Unity says that the races are different and distinct but that they can cooperate and be united in pursuit of a common purpose."

This is a serious objection, one that reflects the way many of us have come to accept the realities of race. As a result, we cannot imagine more than peaceful coexistence and good working relationships. But by focusing on the story of God and the journey toward new creation, we see that the Christian invitation to reconciliation does not simply point to good collaboration between races. It promises that coexistence can happen in a new community that challenges our previous identities of race, tribe and nation. This is God's dream of a new communion "from every nation, tribe, people and language" worshiping God on the throne and the Lamb who was slain (Rev 7:9 NIV). Standing within this story and within this new future, Christians begin to see how infatuation with race, tribe and nation can be idolatry. In other words, the gift of God's story calls us both to a journey beyond reconciling the races as such and to a serious determination to name and resist the privileges, ungodly desires, patterns of life, identities and loyalties that have come to be regarded as normal simply because they are part of our racial, cultural, national or tribal identity.

But aren't differences good? Aren't they a gift created by God? Why would an invitation into the story of new creation seek to overcome the differences that are part of God's creation?

There is nothing in what we have said that denies or minimizes the gifts of difference. We all are created different. In fact, according to the story of creation in Genesis, what God declares good about creation is in part the harmony God creates between different creatures. Far from denying difference, the biblical story acknowledges and affirms both natural and historical differences between peoples. But after the Fall, the gift of difference becomes disfigured and fragile, leading to all sorts of rivalry, divisions and wars between peoples. Our Christian story points us to Pentecost, where differences are not dissolved but restored to their proper order through a new communion in which "we hear them in our own tongues speaking of the mighty deeds of God" (Acts 2:11). Standing at Pentecost, we learn to appreciate what Paul says in Galatians 3:27-28: "For all of you who were baptized into Christ have clothed yourselves with Christ. There is neither Jew nor Greek, slave nor free, male nor female, for you are all one in Christ Jesus" (NIV).

In the stories of Acts, we see Paul deeply immersed in local cultures and colors. He did not suddenly become naive about differences. Instead he proclaimed a powerful story in diverse synagogues and marketplaces—a story that rendered the identities of Greek or Jew, male or female far less interesting. From a Christian point of view, reconciliation is about exploring the biblical story for examples, images, metaphors, practices and ways of living that make our identities as Jew or Greek, American or African, black or white, Korean or Mexican less interesting. Not that there is anything wrong with eating *kimchi* or cheering on your country's soccer team or listening to country and western music. Cultural practices can be wonderful things. Our point is simply this: we must learn where cultural resources and differences can be celebrated and affirmed and where their affirmation becomes a way to obscure or even resist God's plan of building a new and genuine communion of people with diverse histories— the communion Pentecost foreshadows.

For me (Chris) the dinner table that our Antioch Community shared in Jackson remains the metaphor for this vision of life together. Each night for twelve years, anywhere from ten to twenty of us gathered for dinner—white and black, rich and poor, welfare mother and soccer mom, the guest just released from prison and the guest just graduated from Harvard, know-it-all college volunteers and rebellious neighborhood teenagers. Over the flurry of food being passed and animated conversations, the clear lines between identities were blurred, and it became pretty obvious where each person could be celebrated and where each person needed some growing up. Most of all, it was obvious how much we needed one another to become all that Christ was calling us to be. When someone showed up unannounced, our motto was "There's always room for one more."

The practice of making room for one more opens us to genuine communion in a world of difference. In setting the Pentecost table, Christians not only bear witness to the gift of reconciliation we have received from God; we also become ambassadors of God's new creation to a broken and divided world.

A RADICAL REDEFINITION OF JUSTICE

In a similar manner, the biblical story both inspires a search for justice and provides a radical redefinition of justice in our conversation with the world. Within the biblical story, the Christian discovers a constant call for justice on behalf of the weak and forgotten. In the biblical tradition, justice is an aspect of God's *shalom,* a notion that carries with it the idea of completeness, soundness, well-being and prosperity, and includes every aspect of life—personal, relational and national. Moreover, because shalom arises out of covenant relationship and companionship with God, holiness and righteousness are integral to the meaning and practice of justice.

In view of this notion of shalom, the prophets constantly call for justice. But for the biblical authors and prophets, justice makes little sense outside the story of God and of Israel's invitation to be God's particular people. Because they bear the holy name of a just God, Israel is called to "do justice, to love kindness, and to walk humbly with your God" (Mic 6:8). It is as if the prophets are saying, "Without this particular covenant relationship with God, justice is an empty claim." Perhaps this is why the meaning of justice has become so highly contested in our time. Without a shared story and vision of life, society as a whole cannot agree on what justice means.

Drawing attention to the story of God not only makes the call for justice urgent, it also makes it obvious that there can be no justice without reconciliation—and certainly no reconciliation without justice. Both are integral to the journey toward a new creation. In this dynamic journey, not only justice and peace but also truth and mercy meet, as the psalmist notes (see Ps 85:10-11). But even more significantly, in this dynamic meeting place where "truth springs from the earth and righteousness looks down from heaven" (v. 11), the very nature and meaning of *justice* comes to be radically redefined. It is this radical meeting or communion that Acts 2 and 4 speak about as a fresh Pentecost in which "the believers were one in heart and mind," (4:32 NIV) and "all those who had believed were together and had all things in common; and they began selling their property and possessions and were sharing them with all, as anyone might have need" (2:44-45). And elsewhere in Acts: "for there was not a needy person among them, for all who were owners of land or houses would sell them and bring the proceeds of the sales and lay them at the apostles' feet, and they would be distributed to each as any had need" (4:34-35).

These early Christians did not start out with a quest for justice. Rather, they were captured by a fresh story of God's new

Pentecost, and as they were drawn into this story and its communion, they found themselves practicing a far more radical version of justice than they could ever have imagined.

We could go on and on, naming other gifts that Scripture offers in shaping and sustaining the journey of reconciliation. But it is clear enough that reconciliation is not in the first place an activity or set of attitudes but an invitation into a story. Reconciliation names God's story of creation, which is at the same time a promise of restoration. Restoration takes the form of a journey—God's journey to realize that promise in us. To be drawn into the story of Scripture is to join this journey toward new creation. The more we are drawn into this story and journey, the more we are able to catch glimpses of the future. The more we see, the more readily we discover how our current lives, desires, commitments and patterns of life both resist and are being transformed into that vision of God's shalom. "We know that when he appears, we shall be like him, for we shall see him as he is" (1 Jn 3:2 NIV).

5

The Discipline of Lament

*I*n our work leading up to the reconciliation track of the 2004 Lausanne Forum for World Evangelization in Thailand, we traveled to Rwanda. We went to spend a week with ten international Christian leaders, all pursuing reconciliation in historical conflicts across the world, from Korea to South Africa to the United States. It was ten years after the Rwandan genocide, when over 800,000 people were slaughtered during one hundred days of intimate killing, often neighbor killing neighbor. Yet prior to the genocide, Rwanda was considered one of the best-evangelized countries in Africa.

With this seeming contradiction in mind, we came to Rwanda to think together about faithful Christian witness in a divided world. We wanted to reflect in a place where the memory of trauma and violence was fresh and where the church was clearly part of the story of brokenness.

On our first morning in Kigali, we took a bus from our hotel to the city's genocide memorial. Our guide took us to a huge slab of concrete. At first, we didn't know where we were standing. The slab was over a mass grave. Buried underneath it were *two hundred and fifty thousand bodies*—all killed in Kigali alone. Inside an open area at the end, we saw fresh stacks of caskets. Ten years after the genocide, bodies were still being discovered in places from mass graves to latrines. All the killing had happened amid explosive church growth.

Our shock deepened inside the building. We walked through graphic exhibits with stories and video of what happened, displays of bloodstained clothing of the dead along with the simple things people were carrying as they were killed on a road or in the churches that became slaughterhouses. We heard stories of pastors, priests and massive numbers of baptized Christians participating in genocide. And we heard survivors talk about how the world was silent: the United States, the United Nations, African nations, as well as the worldwide church. As we traveled through the exhibit, a Rwandan woman and a young man went through at the same time. From time to time the woman began to weep and wail. The young man tried to console her, but she could not hold back her tears.

After about an hour, our group slowly filed out of the memorial; each of us was drawn to quiet places around a flowing fountain in front. All we could hear was the sound of gurgling water.

We had been involved in reconciliation initiatives throughout our lives. Indeed, many would have called us reconciliation experts. But we had no words. At the genocide memorial in Kigali, we had only silence and tears.

OUR FIRST LANGUAGE IN A BROKEN WORLD

The first language of the church in a deeply broken world is not strategy, but prayer. The journey of reconciliation is grounded in a call to see and encounter the rupture of this world so truthfully that we are literally slowed down. We are called to a space where any explanation or action is too easy, too fast, too shallow—a space where the right response can only be a desperate cry directed to God. We are called to learn the anguished cry of *lament*.

Lament is the cry of Martin Luther King Jr. from his kitchen table in Montgomery after hearing yet another death threat: "Lord, I'm down here trying to do what's right. . . . But Lord, I must confess that I'm weak now, I'm faltering. I'm losing my courage. Now, I am afraid. . . . I am at the end of my powers. I have nothing left. I've come to the point where I can't face it alone."[1]

It was not a cry in isolation but rather a tradition King had learned from generations of African American families who were literally torn apart by slavery. The cry of lament had been passed down to him in the music of the Christian spiritual, "Sometimes I feel like a motherless child, a long way from home. . . . Sometimes I feel like I'm almost gone, a long way from home."

Lament is the cry of the psalmists of Israel in exile who, feeling abandoned by God, demanded, "Where are you, Lord?" Or the psalmists who were bothered by God's remarkably bad sense of timing: "Why are you taking so long?" "The poor are being crushed. The wicked are winning. Don't you see it?" The twin sisters of Psalms are prayers of praise and lament, and they are always walking hand in hand, sometimes singing, sometimes crying.

Lament is not despair. It is not whining. It is not a cry into a void. Lament is a cry directed to God. It is the cry of those who see the truth of the world's deep wounds and the cost of seeking peace. It is the prayer of those who are deeply disturbed by the way things are. We are enjoined to learn to see and feel what the psalmists see and feel and to join our prayers with theirs. The journey of reconciliation is grounded in the practice of lament.

The call to lament finds its way into so much of Scripture—Psalms, Jeremiah, Lamentations and the Gospels in particular. It shows up in the writings of faithful witnesses throughout the church's history. Over and again, lament teaches us about both what must be learned and what must be unlearned in order to live well in a broken world. If we are to participate in God's plan to reconcile all things in Jesus Christ, we must begin to listen to this cry.

A VOICE HEARD IN RAMAH: REFUSING TO BE CONSOLED

The Gospel of Matthew is framed by bookends of murder and death—one at the beginning of Jesus' story and one near the end. From these places come two agonizing cries of lament. The first cry is from a grief-stricken mother. The second is from the anguished Son of God, dying on the cross: "My God, my God, why have you forsaken me?" (Mt 27:46).

An extraordinary statement is included in the first story at the beginning of Matthew. The mothers of Bethlehem are weeping because their innocent young sons have been slaughtered by the fearful King Herod, who seeks to destroy the boy Jesus. Evoking the image of Rachel from the words of Jeremiah, Matthew gives voice to their grief:

> A voice is heard in Ramah,
> Lamentation and bitter weeping
> Rachel is weeping for her children;
> She refuses to be comforted for her children,
> Because they are no more. (Jer 31:15)

The voice from Ramah *refuses to be consoled.* These are profound words in a world full of easy ways of consoling ourselves. Rachel's cry refuses to spiritualize, explain away, ignore or deny the depth and truth of suffering in this world. She rejects soothing words and "can't we all just get along" sentiments. Her refusal takes seriously the rupture and wounds of the world as well as the deep cost of seeking healing. It is a protest against the world as it is and the brokenness that seems so inevitable. Rachel allows the truth to shake her to the very core. And she is remembered for this.

The mourning from Ramah shapes reconciliation as a journey that involves learning about truth, cost and conversion. Lament calls us into a fundamental journey of transformation. If we are to follow the path this practice lays out for us, we have to unlearn three things: speed, distance and innocence.

ATTENDING TO WOUNDS: UNLEARNING SPEED

Our world is captivated by speed. We want to abolish world hunger or solve the AIDS crisis in Africa. And we want to do it fast. To be valid, hope has to make the headlines, have sweeping ambitions, pack stadiums, make its way onto television or produce miracles and prosperity. Campaigns organize around grand promises of "Overcoming Violence" and "Ending Poverty." Even Christianity's growth is measured by numbers of people converted and churches planted. The faster all this happens, the better.

In the field of professional peacebuilding is a widespread "product guarantee": if we learn the right skills, reconciliation will progress with big, visible and certain results. Peacemaking becomes a form of engineering: "Pull this lever, push that button, and here is the certain progress that will happen toward peace."

We cannot forget Karen, the Duke Divinity student who arrived starry-eyed to serve at the L'Arche Daybreak community near Toronto, one of our Teaching Communities. An international organization, it has a great deal of wisdom to share about building communities of reconciliation. L'Arche knows what it takes to sustain over the long haul communities between the disabled and those who are not. Karen was excited to learn from the "experts."

But soon Karen saw bitter divides between some of the staff—the very people she had come to learn from. Over the course of her summer internship, she learned what L'Arche has learned: the more intensely we engage the divides of this world at the places of pain, the more the truth about what is wrong with us comes to the surface. The more we learn to lament, the more we see the need for time to grow, forgive and learn how to love. And if it takes time for just two people to engage that journey, how does that speak to the wider challenges of transformation?

Lament views speed with pessimism. Lament slows reconciliation down because it sees the challenge of transformation not from the top but from the margins—indeed from the bottom. Lament teaches us to see the world from the standpoint of murder in Ramah, exile in Babylon, crucifixion outside Jerusalem, mass graves in Kigali, abandoned people in the New Orleans Superdome after Hurricane Katrina—even from a place as small as a long marriage falling apart while both husband and wife feel powerless to stop it. Transformation looks very different from the bottom.

The more global reconciliation becomes, the more self-assured it is. The more local, the more slow and fragile. Here is where the big "product guarantee" about producing peace meets the words of Jeremiah and the danger of dealing superficially with brokenness: "They dress the wound of my people as though it were not serious. 'Peace, peace,' they say, when there is no peace" (Jer 6:14 NIV).

Speed meets a wall when reconciliation is measured by what is nearest to us—when we see the task as being reconciled within our own homes, families and congregations. Somehow the world can be so busy talking about a global vision for overcoming violence, yet we cannot fix the marriages in our own churches or find healing with an alienated relative or even overcome our own anger toward those who have wounded us.

Every city has its forgotten communities, its geographies that are avoided at all costs. These concentrated places of highest poverty, violence, family disintegration and incarceration hold a great truth within them. Those who have lived and labored for decades in these places know the true pace and fragility of transformation. For every step forward, it often feels like one step back.

It seems odd. We know from experience the difficulty and sacrifice it is to attempt to "end" poverty and violence, even in a single village or neighborhood. Yet grand global plans can be pronounced for both by 2020. Our point is not that lives cannot change in significant ways. They can and they do. But we must learn to see how forgotten communities reveal the true depth of trauma in our world. Lament in local places is a reminder of the long journey to tear down walls and become different people. It prepares us for the slow, daily work by which authentic transformation happens over time.

This is where speed also meets the wall of history and points to the danger of reconciliation without memory—the temptation to forget the wounds of history. Lament calls us to engage the past seriously and to take on the challenge of remembering well. Our friend David Porter, director of the Centre for Contemporary Christianity in Belfast, has labored for decades amid the troubles of Protestant-Catholic division and violence. He argues that it takes as many years to build the peace as it does to create conflicts—and adds that Northern Ireland's troubles were hundreds of years in the making. Lament resists confident talk of ending violence or achieving reconciliation. The best we can do is *pursue* peace and reconciliation. Political settlements do great good when they are genuine. Yet reconciliation is not merely a political end to conflict, or mediation without healing.

A friend of ours recounted an experience he had while working with an international group of Christian missionaries on a plan to combat poverty. During a meeting, one participant suggested it might be helpful to invite some poor people into the process to help the group think more deeply about how to lift people out of poverty. Another participant quickly disagreed. "That would just slow us down," he said.

He was exactly right. But maybe slowing down is what we need. So often we prefer to work superficially and move quickly to "solutions" that only mask our brokenness. Lament calls us to unlearn the habits of speed.

GOING TO RAMAH: UNLEARNING DISTANCE

Closely related to the problem of speed is the problem of distance from suffering. The bookends of lament in Matthew's Gospel press us to come close to particular places—to stand at Ramah beside Rachel, at Calvary beside Jesus. Lament forces us to see the horror of killing and dying there, to feel disturbed by the cries of abandonment and to understand what is at stake in coming alongside and tarrying with pain in concrete places and people.

Learning to lament does not happen anywhere, but *somewhere*. Like real estate, lament is about location, location, location.

The lament of Israel's psalmist erupts from Babylon, not the Promised Land. "Sometimes I feel like a motherless child" cannot be truthfully felt and sung by just anyone, anywhere. It must be felt and remembered from the location where it originated—the social margins of America during slavery. Cries and prayers of lament come from the afflicted, not the comfortable. Lament is the language of people and places who know they are in crisis and not in control.

At a Duke Divinity School forum after the September 11, 2001, attacks, Old Testament professor Ellen Davis cautioned that prayers of lament in Scripture were not written by the world's powerful but by those at the margins who knew they were not in control. While the loss of 9/11 was horrific, Ellen warned that America, with its great military might, should not turn the psalmists' words into the nation's words.

Why are those who are named "oppressed," "poor" and "the least of these" so prominent throughout Scripture? Perhaps to show us that God draws very near to the most vulnerable—not because they're any less sinful, but because they are the most sinned against. They are the ones most likely to be lamenting. By telling the truth about brokenness, we too learn to lament. When we draw near to those who are most sinned against, our call is not first to "make a difference" but to allow the pain of that encounter to disturb us.

We know a young woman who graduated from an Ivy League school and came to study at Duke Divinity School on a prestigious scholarship. She had big plans to lead a justice movement from within the church and become the "female Martin Luther King." During her studies, though, she got involved with the Rutba House community, a small group of Christians who live an undramatic but intentionally engaged life in Walltown, one of Durham's most marginalized neighborhoods. Getting to know people who struggled with their lives against poverty, racism and addiction, she experienced a transformation. In her own words, she gave up on "master plans." She decided she needed to change as much as the people she thought she was helping, so she decided to move into the neighborhood and spend the rest of her life there.

WE ARE PART OF THE PROBLEM: UNLEARNING INNOCENCE
Another way we resist the voice from Ramah is in our tendency to think of ourselves as an innocent solution delivering help to places of human need and conflict. We want to believe that the church is the answer to our world's problems. Yet the truth about Christianity and the landscape of brokenness is always a complex story of both faithfulness and tragedy.

A friend from Rwanda, referring to the genocide in his country, told us, "The church was *here* when all of this was happening. Christians—even priests—joined in the killing. But where is the church to which God entrusted the ministry of reconciliation? Where is *that* church?"

The church was here when all of this was happening. This could be said not only of Rwanda, but also of other deeply "Christian" geographies from Catholics and Protestants in Northern Ireland to South Africa during apartheid. Christians are guilty of intensifying brokenness in many places. We have so often reproduced society rather than offering a witness to it.

On the U.S. landscape, forty years after legal desegregation, where do the trajectories of America's racial history live on most deeply? Not in the well-integrated military or the workplace or the local mall, but in the ongoing, de facto segregation of the Christian church. Ninety percent of white Christians continue to worship in all-white congregations and 90 percent of African-American Christians in all-black congregations, and everyone plays along as if this were normal. The grip of racial self-sufficiency prevails with hardly a whimper of protest from either side. The trajectories of America's racial history have become so embedded in the DNA of the American church that we think of a segregated sabbath as a kind of biological fact.

This is why learning to see and name the truth about the brokenness of the church itself is such an achievement. Otherwise "the way things are" is accepted as exactly that: the natural, acceptable and even inevitable way things have to be.

The more we become intimate with a terrain of profound difference and division, the longer we remain there, the more it reveals our complicity and how much we resist transformation. Learning lament involves not only seeing the church as broken but also seeing our own complicity, how "I" am also part of the problem.

Jean Vanier often tells the story of how, when he first invited two institutionalized men with severe disabilities to come live with him, he was eager to make life better for them. He wanted to serve them, to help them integrate into society. But the daily reality of shared life revealed to Vanier that his new friends did not want to change at the pace or in the ways he desired. What is more, their resistance made him angry. And his anger exposed a deep desire to control. Nothing in Vanier's original vision of "helping" had called him into question. Ministry, he had thought, was all about changing *them*. In time, however, he learned that *he* needed to change too.

The tendency toward triumphalism erodes our capacity to be self-critical. This raises, once again, the problem of starting with the "what do we do?" question. The problem with this question is that it never interrogates the "we." But we need to be questioned—even broken—so that we might be transformed.

LAMENT AS A SHATTERING

Lament in Scripture teaches us that there is nothing romantic about reconciliation. We do not see the depth of our captivity. We prefer reconciliation without repentance. Our desires for speed, distance and innocence run deep. They will not go away without a fight, and that fight is inevitably costly. To lament is to become gripped by the truth of the rupture and the high cost of seeking reconciliation. To learn to lament is to be broken.

The ordinary places of conversion are spaces where fondly held desires and dreams have been shattered. Learning to lament is nothing less than entering a way of dying to self that is at the very heart of the journey of reconciliation. On this way we travel with Jesus to Golgotha, saying, "Not my will, but your will be done." To learn to lament is to see our own visions of transformation shattered on the rocks of the truth about the world's deep rupture and how we ourselves are part of the brokenness.

The people of El Salvador remember Archbishop Oscar Romero as a martyr who gave his life standing up for justice and the poor. But he was not elected archbishop because of his radical politics. Quite the opposite: Romero was chosen as a safe academic who had a consistent record for supporting the status quo. After he was elected, however, the Salvadoran military shot his friend from seminary, Father Rutillio Grande, who had been organizing the poor in a rural parish. After receiving the news of his friend's death, Romero drove through the night to the little town of Aguilares, where his friend lay dead. Those who knew Romero said he was never the same after that night. His worldview shattered by the murder of his friend, Romero began to speak out against his country's repressive government. His old way of being in the world would not work anymore. Lament had transformed him.

LAMENT AS CONVERSION TOWARD AUTHENTIC HOPE

If lament is a way of dying, it is also the path toward being raised into something new. To the extent we do not experience a shattering, something new cannot break in. The relationship between lament and hope is crucial.

First, reconciliation without lament cheapens hope. Any hope not based on the truth is not real hope. The vision of God's justice and peace that Romero glimpsed as he stood by his friend's dead body was more radical than any liberation theology he could have learned in a seminary. Any hope that does not require deep sacrifice is impoverished. Lamentation gives birth to a more radical vision of hope.

Second, to be deeply bothered about the way things are is itself a sign of hope. To the extent we are not shattered, we do not hope. There is in lament a desperation—even more, a demand—for something deeper, something beyond, something new. Those who are not easily consoled have entered a place of restlessness. They've opened their hands to accept a different vision. They are now ready to receive a better hope.

Third, it is crucial to remember that lament is not despair or a cry into a void. Lament is a cry directed *to God*. Lament is prayer. In the midst of the struggle against apartheid in South Africa, Desmond Tutu cried out at a friend's funeral, "Why must the cost be so high?" But in the same prayer of lament he also proclaimed, "God, we know you are going to win." Lament is a cry to the only indispensable One. To lament is to recognize that without God intervening, there can be no reconciliation.

Finally, then, through lament we come to that hard place of knowing that we cannot "achieve" reconciliation. It is always a gift from God. The New Testament calls that gift *metanoia*—a turning, a transformation, a conversion. Lament shapes reconciliation as a long and costly journey that is impossible without receiving the gifts God offers—forgiveness, the promise that our sacrifice is worth it, the patience to stay in an agonizing place and wait for God's reply.

WAYS TO ENGAGE THE DISCIPLINE OF LAMENT: PILGRIMAGE, RELOCATION, CONFESSION

Lament is a discipline in the sense that the book of Hebrews speaks of: "No discipline seems pleasant at the time, but painful. Later on, however, it produces a harvest of righteousness and peace for those who have been trained by it" (Heb 12:11 NIV). Lament is a painful training toward the beauty of seeing what peace truly is and bearing that different vision of peace to the world.

Three ways to learn and engage the discipline of lament are pilgrimage, relocation and public confession. Each of these respective practices offers resources for unlearning speed, distance and innocence.

The practice of *pilgrimage* is a way of unlearning speed. For a number of years, the Office of Black Church Studies at Duke Divinity School, directed by Tiffney Marley, has led students and others on two-week "Pilgrimages of Pain and Hope" to places such as South Africa, Brazil, Rwanda and Uganda, and our own city of Durham. These journeys were inspired by South African pastor Trevor Hudson, whose first pilgrimage simply took his white South African parishioners a few miles across Johannesburg for the first time to live and be present for a few days among the black people of Soweto.

Through a profound rhythm of journeying, encountering sites

of pain and hope, engaging the history and culture, serving and being present with those on the margins, worshiping, resting and reflecting (a critical piece often overlooked on traditional "mission trips"), pilgrims are slowly confronted by a different world that begins to interrupt their own. Pilgrimage is a posture very different from mission. The goal of a pilgrim is not to solve but to search, not so much to help as to be present. Pilgrims do not rush to a goal, but slow down to hear the crying. They are not as interested in making a difference as they are in making new friends. The pace is slower, more reflective.

Pilgrims set out not so much to assist strangers but to eat with them. They journey in the wisdom about transformation held in the Rwandan proverb "If you cannot hear the mouth eating, you cannot hear the mouth crying." There are so many efforts to make a difference that do not make *us* different. It is not the people who paint a house in a strange place but rather the people who make friends and are transformed who make the deeper difference over the long haul. Pilgrims return home as new people. Changed by their journeys, they change the world where they live.

The practice of *relocation,* of taking our very bodies to the hard places and tarrying long enough to be disturbed, is a way of un-learning distance. Forty people die every year from gun violence in Durham. A number of years ago Marcia Owen, the director of the Religious Coalition for a Nonviolent Durham, began taking the time to find out who was murdered, to seek out their loved ones and to organize vigils at the sites of the killings. For each of the hundreds of killings since then, without fail, this restless white woman and many others with her have gathered at the site of the killing with the victim's loved ones and neighbors to pray and cry out.

These deaths no longer make the headlines in Durham. But Marcia and her friends continue to go to the forgotten places to mourn with those who mourn. As they do so, they keep disturbing Durham. They keep joining hands across the tracks to name the crisis. They keep proclaiming that this killing is not normal or inevitable. They keep relocating themselves to the hard places of truth. They keep demanding that the church not become complacent. They keep looking up from that ground to demand God's attention. They keep disturbing and cajoling. They join the anguished mothers of Durham who refuse to be consoled when their sons and daughters are killed.

The practice of *public confession* is a way of unlearning innocence. As we learn to go out of our way to draw near and tarry with the pain of the world in concrete places, the challenge is to keep naming the truth, keep being disturbed, keep remembering the awful depth of brokenness. The prayers of lament in Psalms were public prayers, intended to be read and inserted into the corporate life of worship. They have been read communally throughout church history, in the daily office of the monasteries and the weekly worship of parishes. It is critical that we learn how to pray like this, bringing these prayers into public worship in a way that helps us tell the truth and confess in explicit relationship to the brokenness of our own contexts.

What might this look like in a city like Durham? In the context of public prayer for a church that is distant from the places of death across the tracks, we might take the time to name and remember those who were killed and the ones who killed them in our city last week. We might remember their loved ones and join our cries with theirs. We might confess that we have not attended to this brokenness or demanded that God pay attention. With this kind of public prayer and confession, the three marks of lament—truth, cost and conversion—become quite real and visible.

This will be unsettling, but that is exactly the point. Praying this way creates a very uncomfortable place where we learn to tell the truth in public. But it may also give us the courage to keep staying in the journey when we do not know the way, when we are in over our heads, when we are not in control of where we are headed. Lament teaches us to look to God for the resources to go on. After unlearning speed, distance and innocence, we learn to be present in a different way to a broken world.

One of our divinity students, Susan, worked a summer in Durham as a hospital chaplain at an intensive care unit for newborn children. One day a family from Africa lost their baby, who had been in the hospital's care for four months. The mother was devastated, lost in her grief. Susan prayed with her. Afterward she watched as two nurses came to the mother and asked if she wanted them to help her clean the baby. Together they removed the tubes. As the mother and nurses stood over the baby and washed her, they began singing over her lifeless body. They cried and expressed intense emotions of grief. The nurses did not avoid the mother's grief and pain. They did not tell her it was in God's plan. They did not try to cheer her up. They gave her a beautiful outlet for her raw emotion.

To learn to lament is to become people who stay near to the wounds of the world, singing over them and washing them, allowing the unsettling cry of pain to be heard. The question Susan pressed about her experience is the transformation to which lament calls us: "Are we ready to become that vulnerable?"

6

Hope in a Broken World

*L*ament and death frame Matthew's Gospel. To forget this is to take the wounds of the world too lightly.

But lament and death are neither the first nor the last word of that Gospel. The story begins with the gift of God's Son coming into the world and ends with Jesus' resurrection and ascension into heaven. The gospel story begins and ends in the hope of incarnation and resurrection. Without this larger vision of hope, we perish.

Yet hope is difficult in our world because it is often confused with optimism and success. This is why we must learn to lament before turning to hope. In the call to lament, we have already said a great deal about the nature of authentic hope. When we see what needs to be unlearned about speed, distance and innocence, we also uncover what needs to be unlearned about hope. Reconciliation without lament cheapens hope. We must refuse the consolations of cheap hope.

Scripture points out to us that the hope God brings is radical and distinct:

See, I am doing a new thing!
Now it springs up; do you not perceive it?
I am making a way in the desert
and streams in the wasteland. (Is 43:19 NIV)

God's "way in the desert and streams in the wasteland" are not easily seen or perceived. God is always planting seeds of hope, always doing something new and fresh—but not in the ways we expect, look for or even desire. When the world's desperate search for success masks a desire to short-circuit the journey of reconciliation, we fail to recognize and live by God's more radical vision of hope and transformation. This vision is nothing less than the hope of enemies and strangers becoming friends and of all becoming God's companions. It is a vision of hope grounded in the unseen.

HOPE IS GROUNDED IN AND ANTICIPATES
THINGS NOT SEEN

Training in Christian hope doesn't start with results. It starts with remembering. Whenever we go to the table of bread and wine to receive God's gifts or open the Bible and read together, we are drawn into a vision of God's "new thing," which does not hold hope hostage to the rules of cause and effect.

The remarkably different lives of the cloud of witnesses in Hebrews 11 were not grounded in the visible, but in the unseen. They had a concrete vision of beyond: "By faith our ancestors received approval . . . now faith is the assurance of things hoped for, the conviction of things not seen" (Heb 11:2, 1 NRSV). They were gripped by a vision of "a better country," believing that the way things are is not the way things have to be. These convictions about "things not seen" did not lead these witnesses into complacency but reshaped their very actions and lives as restless "strangers and foreigners on the earth" (v. 13 NRSV). Risking his reputation, Noah built an ark. Risking his life, Moses fled privilege with Pharaoh, then returned to confront him. Surrendering his homeland, Abraham embarked on a journey into unknown lands. Convictions about "things not seen" inspired actions toward a new identity that were often disturbing to those comfortable with the status quo.

Nelson Mandela's life in jail on Robben Island during the terror of white supremacy is a sign of this new identity within an unseen "better country." Looking back, it seems easy to name the "steps to success" by which people overcame apartheid in South Africa. But during those decades, the spirit of grace and acts of hospitality with which Mandela treated his jailers was scandalous. In spite of no apparent change, he lived as if things were already different. Mandela lived as if he and his white captors were already living in a new South Africa.

What makes it worth living as if things have already changed? It's not the guarantee that things will be different now. Injustice may endure for years. But we have been seduced and transformed by things hoped for, things not seen. This is the ground of Christian hope.

HOPE PRESSES TOWARD A NEW PLACE OF FRIENDSHIP

"See, I am doing a new thing!" God says (Is 43:19 NIV). What does hope look like in God's vision of the new?

In the midst of violence, it is profoundly new to desire a truce with one's enemy. Achieving this truce is where the social will toward newness often ends. The settlement happens, the open hostilities end, and the funding dries up. But enemies remain distant and wounds become hidden. It is one thing to desire a truce with the stranger and enemy, but quite another to desire friendship with him or her.

While Americans may be living post-desegregation, we have settled at best for integration toward a kind of multicultural consumerism where everyone is free to pursue the American dream of economic prosperity. But the biblical vision of hope with respect to brokenness and conflict is indelibly shaped by the strange language and stories of *shalom*, *koinonia* and *metanoia*. Christian hope is intimately connected to these images of flourishing, shared life and deep transformation with repentance seen in the stories of Pentecost, Peter's encounter with Cornelius at Caesarea, strangers becoming companions at Antioch, "neither Jew nor Greek . . . " in Galatians, and "one new humanity" in Ephesians. In short, Christian hope arches toward strangers and enemies becoming friends.

In the last chapter we pointed to the significance of communities at the margins as locations of lament that help us to see the truth of how divided our society remains. Yet if lament is a way of dying, it is also the path toward being raised into something new.

Hope looks like what Anglican Archbishop Rowan Williams has called "communities of resurrection." Such communities are birthed as an intentional response to an enormous social gap. They show us that for which we should pray and yearn. They teach us that in a highly racialized society, peace looks like African Americans and white Americans praising God together.

But these communities also show what is possible. Their significance is as "signs" pointing to a different life that can interrupt the trajectories of alienation, injustice and separation. With their more radical vision, these communities point toward a future not yet realized. They prove that neither distance nor assimilation is the best choice. They point to the need to create spaces and places that become schools for conversion.

Our friend Jonathan Wilson-Hartgrove runs an alternative seminary that invites people to learn about "Christianity as a Way of Life." The school doesn't have buildings (which keeps costs pretty low). Neither does it have full-time faculty. Instead this School for Conversion invites people to come and see "new monastic" communities of intentional Christian discipleship.[1] Students study Scripture with their host community. Together, the groups prepare meals and eat. They talk about theology and even read some good books. But more than that, they participate in an experiment with the kind of life God makes possible. They are learning that discipleship is about being transformed by a new place of friendship.

HOPE EMBRACES THE SIGNIFICANCE OF THE SMALL

Over and over Scripture points us to hope below the radar in stories about yeast and mustard seeds, a few fish and five loaves, foot washings and the welcoming of strangers. Bread and wine are very ordinary, yet in Holy Communion God offers them to us as the body and blood of Christ. Water, too, is very ordinary, yet in baptism it makes us children of God. Scripture slows us down to notice and celebrate God's power to nourish the world through the small, the weak and the ordinary.

Our friend Emmanuel Ndikumana is a Hutu married to a Tutsi in Burundi. As a leader at the university in Bujumbura, he constantly finds himself caught between the Burundi military, dominated by Tutsi, and the predominantly Hutu rebel groups who are fighting the government. But he knows that small things make a difference in the everyday lives of people, so he has formed groups of Hutu and Tutsi students who travel together. When they come to a military checkpoint, the Tutsi students talk with the soldiers. When they come to a rebel roadblock, Hutu student leaders do the talking while the rest of the students carry on with their own conversations. This way, they are able to confuse both the military and rebel fighters.

The Christian vision of hope never disconnects the question of whether we can reconcile the nations from whether we can live in peace and forgiveness with those nearest to us—in our homes, at work, in worship and even on the road. We remember the leader of a high-powered global health initiative who asked how she could claim to fix the world's health problems when she could not even fix the ruptured relationship between her husband and his sister. A single relationship offered her a window into the complexity of human brokenness. But one relationship transformed by the power of God can also give us reason to hope that another world is possible.

For over twenty years, New Song Church and Ministries in the inner-city Sandtown neighborhood of Baltimore has seen the lives of many people deeply changed. Hope is visible in a sparkling new charter school, flourishing Habitat for Humanity homes, Martha's House for people in recovery and an interracial church at the heart of it all. Yet New Song has only touched a few blocks in Baltimore. The "only" is exactly the point. Seeing the transformations that hope requires in a few blocks amid the pain of inner-city Baltimore slows us down to see the difficult, daily work that hope demands in any place. The only way divided lives and communities are deeply transformed into a new way of life together is *slowly*. New Song is not so much a success story as a sign of what hope looks like in the conversion of everyday life into which the story of Scripture inspires us to live.

HOPE REQUIRES REPENTANCE AND CONVERSION

Hope in reconciliation is possible only through that gift the New Testament calls *metanoia*—a turning the other way, a transformation. It is a conversion, but not in the sense of a one-time moment. It is, rather, a long and costly journey with God through which we are constantly being transformed into new life.

Christianity understands the highest good in a broken world to be the transformation of strangers and enemies into friends. The question is, how are our desires to be fundamentally transformed so that we want life together with people who have hurt us? This is a political question. There is much talk about the political dimensions of negotiating conflict. But politics is not chiefly about the realm of government. Day to day, politics is about the deeper questions of discerning the common good and negotiating a life together. Politics is about how the communities we are a part of order (and disorder) our allegiances and identities.

The journey of reconciliation points us toward a politics of repentance, a unique journey in the messy and stubborn "now" of history. On this journey, our disordered desires are transformed toward friendship across lines of estrangement. Hope celebrates small signs of transformation, because the politics of repentance is the accumulation over time of many moments that together amount to lives decisively turned toward the "other."

We marvel to see our friends Moss Nthla, a black South African, and Nico Smith, a white Afrikaner, working together today in a country where apartheid was the norm for so long. Just fifteen years ago, neither of these men could have imagined the end of apartheid, a national Truth and Reconciliation Commission with Desmond Tutu as its leader or the presidency of Nelson Mandela. While it is crucial to note the politics of power behind these achievements, it is just as crucial to see the politics of repentance.

The South African Truth and Reconciliation Commission (TRC) has drawn enormous attention, and people around the world are seeking to replicate it. But the unique gift of the TRC is not that it unveiled the truth about historic injustices, but that it did so within an atmosphere of mercy and forgiveness. This was possible only because Tutu had already been transformed into a man who could not envision the future without forgiveness. In other words, if a new South Africa is not possible without the unique gifts of its TRC, the TRC was not possible without the forgiveness of Tutu— a sort of "X factor" in the South African experience. The formation of such people through repentance is what hope requires.

Without the politics of repentance, those on top may be coerced into change, but they will never be truly transformed. And the victim who gains power is always in danger of becoming the next victimizer.

HOPE BEARS PROPHETIC WITNESS AMID INJUSTICE

The call to embody hope in a journey of repentance is intimately connected to the call for Christians to faithfully bear witness in the world of powers—navigating the messy realities of ruling authorities, economic interests and armed forces that powerfully shape life and loyalties for every human person. We all live in a world of powers.

History cautions us against forms of Christianity that become complicit with evil and injustice. With the exception of the Confessing Church in 1930s Germany, most churches and leaders gradually turned their social existence over to the

Nazi party. Over decades in Rwanda, many church leaders cozied up to government powers during different regimes. Among the bad ways of navigating powers are not only this easy assimilation but also a quietism about power. We are tempted to act as if our faith were something entirely apart from the negotiation of power.

The challenge for Christians is always one of learning the right negotiation between prophetic *presence* on the one hand and prophetic *distance* on the other. Prophetic presence is required to know when and how to speak with boldness. In South Africa in 2005, I (Chris) met Duma Kumalo, one of the Sharpeville Six who was unjustly condemned to death in 1984 for his alleged actions with five others to murder the deputy mayor of Sharpeville. Duma told me that just fifteen hours before his scheduled execution, he was pardoned. With great passion he looked at me and said, "I am literally here alive because of people in your country, because someone intervened."

Yet prophetic distance is also required so as not to give over ultimate loyalty to any ruling party or power. During my time in South Africa, I also met a young, white Afrikaner who grew up steeped with a sacred vision of the superiority of whiteness wrapped tightly around his Christianity. Anyone who opposed apartheid, he said, was seen as a communist. His moment of conversion happened in 1995 while watching TRC proceedings on public television. "I didn't understand apartheid was a lie until 1995," he said. He had to step back and see his country from a distance to see it truly.

The faithful negotiation of prophetic presence and prophetic distance can be costly. There are reasons why many of history's most recent ambassadors for peace have been assassinated—Mahatma Gandhi, Martin Luther King Jr., Anwar Sadat. True peace is not popular. A deeper vision of hope upsets the patterns of power and self-interest.

HOPE TRESPASSES BOUNDARIES AND PLANTS MERCY AMID ANTAGONISM

In the lives of these martyrs for peace, we also see the sign of a deeper vision of hope when people plant seeds of hospitality, mercy and forgiveness across boundaries of antagonism and injustice, without the guarantee that things will change as a result.

After the 1979 Islamic revolution in Iran, ties were cut between the United States and Iranian governments, and three decades of antagonism followed from America's bitter memory of the Iran hostage crisis. But after an earthquake in Iran in 1990, a seed was planted when Mennonite Christians offered assistance. Eventually, workers from the Mennonite Central Committee (MCC) established a quiet presence in Iran via small gestures, living among the Iranian people, building friendships on the streets, setting up health clinics, assisting Iraqi and Afghan refugees, and establishing student exchanges between Canada and Iran. In February of 2007, unexpected fruit came when MCC was invited to organize the first face-to-face meeting of an American delegation with an Iranian president since the bitter break of 1979.

Hope trespasses boundaries in the name of becoming the new creation. In 2006, the Duke Chapel congregation that gathers at Duke University became convinced that their privilege and power had left them too distant from the divides of Durham. Out of this restlessness, leaders at the chapel eventually discovered a welcoming group of strangers not far from campus—neighbors and community leaders who invited them into the West End, a historic African-American neighborhood full of gifts, economic and social challenges, and new Latino immigrants. The chapel commissioned two pastors, Abby and Craig Kocher, to buy a house and move into the West End community. Abby was asked not to start programs, but to walk the streets, pray with people, meet with community leaders and wait to see what doors would open.

A group of Duke undergraduates live in a house in the community each year, and others are trickling in. The journey is young. But it has begun not with public relations, a big splash or a grand vision, but in trespassing boundaries to seek friendship across divides, in the expectation that somehow Duke Chapel will never be the same.

HOPE CELEBRATES JOY AND BEAUTY IN THE URGENCIES OF A BROKEN WORLD

In a world that entices us to put ultimate hope in human activism, a deeper hope develops when we drop everything and take the time for beauty, rest and celebration—to visit a garden, enjoy a friend, love our children well, praise and pray.

Such actions are about far more than recharging our batteries. Beauty, rest and celebration don't just refresh us. They reshape our goals and vision. There is intrinsic good when we do the things that return our hearts and minds and lives to receiving and living by "things not seen." Acts of beauty, joy, praise and stillness before God call us to remember and proclaim that reconciliation is God's work.

A friend told us of visiting a very large religious community with a long history of activism and service. For generations St. Benedict's monastery had built hospitals and sent teachers into public schools. In its early history on the American frontier, it had literally saved the lives of weary travelers with its hospitality. Walking with one of the sisters in the community's beautifully cared for cemetery, our friend asked what the elderly sister loved most about her community. "We do death well," she said. "You should see a funeral here. It's really a beautiful culmination of a life lived in worship of God."

Over time a community like this monastery can transform a place through its service and work, creating space for human life to flourish. But such a community is sustained through small acts of beauty like doing death well. These acts point to a deeper vision that is easily lost in the urgencies of a broken world. They are themselves seeds in this broken world that are just as prophetic as our work for justice and peace.

There is no guarantee that these small seeds will take hold and grow into something beautiful for all the world to see. They could die from lack of water or be choked by weeds. We plant in hope, not certainty. But we plant because we know it is true and right and good. Even as we bend to push the seeds beneath moist soil, we are learning that hope is the patience to work and wait for a future not yet seen.

7

Why Reconciliation
Needs the Church

$\mathscr{T}$he vision of reconciliation outlined in this book needs a
church where real and fragile people embody the gospel. Reconciliation is grounded in a story—the story of God's new creation. We first learn this story from and through the church that
worships God and reads Scripture to remember God's journey
with us. As we do the work of being God's people together, we
begin to see ourselves as companions and fellow travelers on the
journey toward God's new creation. The church is crucial to this
journey, not simply because the journey requires a community to
sustain it, but also because the life, ministry and practices of the
community allow us to catch glimpses of that new communion
into which the journey of reconciliation leads.

Christians learn the language of reconciliation from and
through the community called church. But we also need the

church to form patterns and habits that sustain the journey of reconciliation, even as the church continually reminds us as Christians that this journey is what our life is all about. Without an account of this community of the church, we are back to the dominant image of lone firefighters trying to put out one fire after another in an increasingly violent world.

In this chapter we provide images and metaphors that display what the church is and should be in order to make the account of reconciliation we have outlined above both possible and sustainable.

A SIGN: THE FOOT WASHING AT PATTAYA

At the conclusion of a week of meetings at the Lausanne Forum on World Evangelization in Pattaya, Thailand, in 2004, each of the thirty or so issue groups had an opportunity to give a five-minute report to the general assembly of their recommendations for the future of Christian mission. Our issue group on reconciliation was number twenty-two in a series of presentations. The night before, someone in our group had an idea: instead of a five-minute report, we would do a foot washing to communicate what our group was all about. So when the time for our report came, we set up on the convention floor twelve people with basins and towels. Then as two people narrated what happened in our group during the week, the twelve people washed each other's feet: a Catholic priest, an Orthodox priest and an evangelical pastor; an Israeli and a Palestinian; a black, a white and an Asian American; Hutu and Tutsi; male and female.

At the end of the presentation, the polite silence of the convention hall was interrupted by a standing ovation. But then it was time for another group to present its five-minute report to the assembly. The show had to go on. Looking back, however, we think that interruption of one report after another offered us a glimpse of what the church is called to be: a community on its knees, washing feet across divides.

Of course, we have to acknowledge that the actual reality we live in is much different. We live in a world of war, conflict and genocide inspired by racial, tribal and religious identities. More often than not, the church self-segregates neatly along these dividing lines. Even within the same denomination or congregation, various divisions often fuel battles and animosities. This is the church we know. Without a glimpse of something new like we saw at Pattaya, we might assume that the divisions of race, tribe and nation are not only inevitable, but even normal.

Unless the church is able to be the space where people who share different cultures and histories can receive their common gift and invitation to the same journey, then the church herself becomes just one more actor in the history of division and conflict. Instead of healing the tensions and brokenness of the world, the church can become an epicenter that radiates and intensifies these divisions.

More than a space carved out for dialogue, the church is called to be a people who share a story and a journey. When we met in Pattaya with representatives of people groups from around the world, the first few days were filled with many awkward moments and silences. There did not seem to be a lot that Hutu and Tutsi, Palestinian and Israeli, Americans and Albanians, evangelical and Orthodox had in common. But as we prayed with and for one another, sang and worshiped together, read and reflected on Scripture, listened to each other's stories of pain and hope, a sense of communion—of being fellow travelers—began to emerge. Stefan Stankovic, a young leader from Serbia, said, "This is the first time I have been in the same room with an Orthodox priest or heard one bless something that evangelicals are doing!"

A DEMONSTRATION PLOT

It would be wrong to think of the meeting at Pattaya as "achieving" reconciliation. Foot washing is not our example of how to do reconciliation across different Christian denominations and geographies. We did not meet to fix the many divisions and conflicts represented by the members of our group. And we did not leave feeling we had succeeded in doing so. We came together as a group of theologians and Christian leaders involved in the ministry of reconciliation to reflect on our work. As we did, what was poignantly revealed and confirmed to us in the gesture of foot washing was the nature and mission of the church in reconciliation.

The scene of a divided church on its knees, washing one another's feet, pointed to a communion beyond race, tribe, nation and denomination. The primary task of the church in reconciliation is not to mediate but to point beyond the conflict. New creation directs us beyond radical divisions to an alternative way of living together.

This is the very nature and essence of the church: to exist as the sign of a reality beyond itself. It is not that the church is the new reality. The church's mission is to gesture to this reality beyond us. The promise of new life is what gives the church its uniqueness as well as its challenge—namely, to be an imperfect yet compelling demonstration plot of the new creation we announce.

THE INTERRUPTING CHURCH

The church's freshness always breaks through in the form of an interruption. What made the foot washing at Pattaya such a powerful sign was the fact that it was an interruption to the smooth, methodical, predictable and well-organized program of the convention. The foot washing did not really fit in with the five-minute reports each group was expected to give. It disrupted this flow. But as a result, people felt a fresh wind of the Spirit.

We worry that some might find in our description a beautiful but very quaint view of the church as a community, satisfied with bearing witness to her story but not in conversation with other players and actors. This is not what we are advocating. In fact, there is no way that the interrupting church can be anything but a community that constantly finds itself in crisis, negotiating its existence and message while surrounded by other voices. We must always be in conversation with others. Whether we find ourselves in America, Rwanda or South Africa, the landscape is already controlled by voices that seem far more powerful than our own. Still, our mission is to announce, to point to and to radiate a freshness that draws from somewhere else.

We proclaim a future that is not seen. This is why our interruptions are not limited to a time of conflict but are just as needed during the so-called peaceful times. For the church to be capable of interruption, we must exist as a community that is willing to adjust itself to the constant interruption of the stranger. The church is not only an interrupt*ing* community: we are ourselves always interrupt*ed*.

In 1988 I (Emmanuel) was a newly ordained priest, full of zeal and confidence not only about God's plan for the salvation of the world, but also about my place as God's minister within that divine plan. I was an assistant priest at a busy parish in the middle of Kampala. As I was putting my final touches on the homily for the afternoon mass, I heard a knock on my door.

Before I could answer, a man who must have been in his late twenties opened the door and slumped into one of the chairs. He was sweating, and his eyes were red. I asked if there was anything I could do for him. He did not respond but only stared at me. After an awkward period of silence he blurted out these words: "Father, I have been to the hospital to be tested. I am HIV positive. I am afraid, and I do not know how I will break this news to my wife and my two children."

Then he broke down and cried. I sat with him there, not knowing what to say. When it was time for me to go for mass, I left him in my office. But as I began to read my well-prepared homily for the day, I realized it was flat. It did not make any sense. All I could think of was this man—his face, his fear, his story. Somewhere in the middle of the homily, I found I could not go on. I simply stopped and asked the congregation to pray for the young man whom I had left in my office. I did not even know what to ask them to pray for.

Since that day, every time I think about the challenge of AIDS in Africa, I think about Michael. His presence interrupted my sermon preparation as well as the normal mass on that day in 1988. More than that, though, it always reminds me of our vocation to interrupt the status quo and make sure that the life of the church is somehow good news to people like Michael. Even when we don't know what to do, we can't just go on with business as usual.

THE INTERRUPTED CHURCH

There is a story told by all the evangelists (with varying details), which we need to retell in order to capture its full breadth:

> Now one of the Pharisees was requesting Him to dine with him, and He entered the Pharisee's house and reclined at the table. And there was a woman in the city who was a sinner; and when she learned that He was reclining at the table in the Pharisee's house, she brought an alabaster vial of perfume, and standing behind Him at His feet, weeping, she began to wet His feet with her tears, and kept wiping them with the hair of her head, and kissing His feet and anointing them with the perfume. Now when the Pharisee who had invited Him saw this, he said to himself, "If this man were a prophet He would know who and what

sort of person this woman is who is touching Him, that she is a sinner." (Lk 7:36-39)

This story speaks right to the nature and mission of the church. It confirms that the church is an interrupted gathering of a beloved community. The dinner party is interrupted by the unwelcome presence of a stranger. In fact, it is through this interruption that the beloved community is called to see more clearly that we are not a lifestyle enclave. The community of Jesus is not a spiritual gated community or a ghetto of moral righteousness. Instead the stranger constantly interrupts our life. Hospitality, openness and an ongoing engagement with the stranger are hallmarks of our life together.

Through this interruption our community is able to recover the extravagant love and service that our existence is about. It helps us remember that our life together is always about the very concrete and mundane realities of service—acts as concrete as the tears, jars, oil, hair and feet of this interrupting woman's prophetic witness. We may get excited about committee meetings and programs to end homelessness in our city, but the alternative to homelessness we are called to embody requires the daily work of homemaking. In cooking dinner and making beds with love, men and women alike live the gospel that this woman proclaims with her actions.

We also learn from this story that there is something urgent about the church's ministry that we too often forget. We need the interruption and gift of the stranger to be drawn back into this urgency. Whereas Luke's version of the story does not specify the time when this event takes place, all the other evangelists are careful to note that it was right before the Passover. Seen from this angle, it becomes obvious that the action of the woman at Simon's house is an anticipation of the wider story of the Passion. This interruption happens in the midst of a violent story about the battering of Jesus' body.

In the history of the church, St. Francis's ability to read the signs of his time stands out as an example of the way attention to the wider story enables us to interrupt the powers that be. Looking back at history, we can see that Francis's movement of friars who begged on behalf of the poor coincided with the rise of a money economy and the new merchant class in Europe. Francis interrupted the new economy with a reminder of God's providence. He was able to do this, however, only because he struggled honestly with the question of how to live the gospel faithfully as the son of a cloth merchant. Attending to the question of discipleship in the concrete reality of his own context, Francis started a movement that would transform Christendom.

The anointing at Bethany reminds the beloved community of the wider story in which we always finds ourselves. In relation to the story of the Passion, the anointing at Bethany points us to the gifts of forgiveness, hospitality, service and extravagant care. Only by being a community open to interruption is the church capable of bearing these gifts and thus offering a freshness that goes beyond skills and techniques to a whole way of life, grounded in a story and vision of a beyond.

On Feet, Hair, Jars and Tears:
A Fleshly Account of Reconciliation

It is important to draw attention to *how* the interruption at Bethany (as well as Pattaya) happened. The freshness of the beyond that the church points to is not an abstract or esoteric condition. Rather, it is as concrete, mundane and ordinary as washing feet, planting cabbages, changing diapers, caring for the sick. This is why we cannot think of reconciliation as one particular ministry of the church. The church does not pursue reconciliation as if it were a project. Reconciliation is what happens to the church as she finds herself faithfully and patiently living out a vision of the beyond in her most ordinary, simple and mundane tasks.

In his book *Hope for Rwanda*, Father Andre Sibomana notes how hard it was in the aftermath of genocide to bring Hutu and Tutsi together to talk about, even less agree on, the history of Rwanda. But then he tells of an incident in which he mobilized the people of his parish for the communal work of reconstruction. He recalls how they had to build everything from scratch: gardens, houses, pit latrines. During a break from the work, Sibomana was amazed to see Hutu and Tutsi workers drinking banana beer from the same cup.

Sibomana's experience reminds us that a church interrupted by God's new creation doesn't assume an otherworldly posture. Rather, it finds itself deeply engaged in everyday, mundane realities. Without a thick and material account of church, we may tend to view reconciliation as a spiritual event or a shallow sentiment that involves merely hugs and handshakes. But we see a different reality on the ground. Reconciliation is about killers and their victims' family members taking a break from their common work to drink banana beer from the same cup.

Once the biblical story of reconciliation is recovered, it is easy to see that reconciliation requires an account of the church. In the context of this story, our need for particular skills to help heal the pain of the past, mediate conflict, resist injustice and fight oppression takes on a special significance and urgency.

But this is not isolated work. It is all connected to the invitation to be *"ambassadors* for Christ, as though God were making an appeal through us" (2 Cor 5:20, emphasis added). Ordinarily, the task of being an ambassador involves living in the country where one is placed and engaging the politics of that country while representing the interests of one's own. If we think of new creation as the politics that Christians represent, then the invitation to be ambassadors is to live wherever we find ourselves, to engage the politics of that place from the vantage point of God's new creation and to try to influence that politics through various tactics so that it may increasingly resemble that new creation. This requires us not only to read carefully the history of the places where we dwell, but also to use whatever tactics, gifts and resources we have to advance the politics of new creation.

This is the very meaning of *incarnation*. For, as Paul reminds us, we must "have the same attitude as Christ":

Although He existed in the form of God, [Jesus] did not regard equality with God a thing to be grasped, but emptied Himself, taking the form of a bond-servant, and being made in the likeness of men.

Being found human in appearance as a man, He humbled Himself by becoming obedient to the point of death, even death on a cross. (Phil 2:5-8)

In connection with reconciliation, incarnation means learning to be there in broken places and developing the patience and discipline necessary to stay long enough to see the needs. That is why every time we think about incarnation, we think about Dorothy Day and the Catholic Worker movement she founded. Her testimony of how it all started is very telling:

We were just sitting there talking when lines of people began to form saying, "we need bread." We could not say, "Go, be thou filled." If there were six small loaves and a few fishes, we had to divide them. There was always bread.

We were just sitting there talking and people moved in on us. Let those who can take it, take it. Some moved out and that made room for more. And somehow the walls expanded.

We were just sitting there talking and someone said, "let's all go live on a farm." It was as casual as all that, I often think. It just came about. It just happened.[1]

Day's story confirms the significance of presence. Only because we are "just sitting there" do we feel and see the need.

Only when we're present to the world's brokenness do we ask what is required to respond to the need. Through incarnation, reconciliation ceases to be spectacular and becomes the purpose of our everyday lives.

This is the conviction behind John Perkins's insistence on *relocation* as a crucial component of his "three Rs" vision for Christian community development: relocation, reconciliation and redistribution. Relocation is about the significance of place. The church's presence in broken neighborhoods turns poor people from statistics into friends, reshaping how we see the world. For Perkins, this incarnational presence (relocation) makes possible the reshaping of broken relationships (reconciliation) and fuels the relentless pursuit of justice (redistribution).

From this perspective of incarnational ministry, the work of reconciliation cannot be limited to occasional intervention during conflicts but is about the patterns of everyday life. Reconciliation seeks to endow the practices of ordinary life with a flourishing that more closely reflects God's plan to reconcile all things in Christ. Of course, the particular forms that the struggle for human flourishing takes varies depending on the history and needs of a place. To discern these things, we have to be there.

All we are really saying is that incarnation grounds the ministry of reconciliation in such a way that we learn to read the history, geography and needs of a place. As we do this in the context of God's story, our imaginations are shaped to see what the embodiment of God's promises could look like in our own neighborhoods. Without the story of God pointing to incarnation as both a model and a pattern of Christian living, we can never develop the patience or the skills necessary for the long haul of the Christian journey of reconciliation.

We do not want to glamorize incarnational presence. Nor do we want to suggest that the church's presence is a panacea for the world's brokenness. To be sure, in many places and at different periods of history, the church's presence has been less of a gift and more of a challenge. Instead of being a peaceable and interruptive presence on a landscape of brokenness, the church has often taken on the same patterns and characteristics of its place, sometimes even serving to make things worse.

This is a serious challenge that has no easy answers. In view of the discussion above, it reflects a failure to live faithfully in specific places while representing and pursuing the interests and politics of new creation. Over time, it becomes easy to forget the story and politics of our true home and to try to make the location of assignment "home." How does the church keep this from happening? How can we be at once local and yet foreign, incarnate and yet interruptive, ordinary and yet ever fresh? These are the questions we are called to live into in the seemingly ordinary in-between of this world's broken places.

8

The Heart, Spirit
and Life of Leadership

The story that grounds us, the gifts God offers and the practices of faithfulness we have outlined in this book do not offer a how-to guide for reconciliation. But we hope they stir up a want-to in the hearts of restless people who, like us, know the brokenness of this world and long for it to be healed. A desire for reconciliation is crucial.

And yet desire is not enough. If the church is to live into the vision of reconciliation we've outlined, we need, among other gifts, a unique type of leadership. We have many experts on the terrain of conflict, but not many leaders. Experts direct from a distance. They focus on skills and how-tos. The goal of the expert is conflict resolution or a cessation of hostilities. They offer techniques, skills and a clear beginning and end to their involvement in the process. The struggle is not their struggle. Once things start to go well—or too badly—they withdraw.

Good Christian leadership radiates a very different presence in a broken world. Such leadership reminds the church of a different story and politics—the loyalty to Christ's lordship over all things, which is to shape our whole lives. In a world where loyalty to Christ is constantly contested, the ministry of reconciliation calls forth a specific kind of everyday leader who is able to unite a deep vision with the concrete skills, virtues and habits necessary for the long and often lonesome journey of reconciliation. Wherever we find hope in a broken world, we see the significance of such everyday leaders.

Unlike experts, Christian leaders are both inspired by a vision of God's future and grounded in the thick stubbornness of the now. They have made the conflict their struggle. They are on a journey whose end they envision but whose realization is beyond them. They know the journey will be costly but that the victory belongs to God.

We want steps, blueprints and plans. But there is no road map for leaders on the journey of reconciliation. They travel a particular terrain, history and context, navigating toward the new creation and a future not yet realized. There will be many chapters in such a journey, chapters we cannot anticipate or prepare for in advance. The challenge is to keep fresh and continue growing along the way.

Even so, leaders do not travel alone. A "cloud of witnesses" goes with us, and there is much to learn from the lives and journeys of those who have gone before us. We must never put the communion of saints like those discussed in this book outside our reach and our world. While few may ever approach their stature, they are signs of the Holy Spirit at work in the world, and their lives point our own lives in the right direction.

What we see in their lives is that leadership in the ministry of reconciliation is more about a heart and soul than a strategy—a unique kind of heart, spirit and life that inspires and sustains this difficult ministry over the long haul. What does this unique heart, spirit and life of everyday leaders look like in the journey of reconciliation?

RESPONDING TO A GAP

Reflecting on the challenge of leading the L'Arche communities after many decades, Jean Vanier points to an ordinariness that emerges in learning to tell the story of how ministry begins. Writes Vanier,

> We do not have all the answers. But the vital thing is to remember and to tell the story of how it all began. And the story begins with a huge gap of injustice and pain. It is the gap between the so-called "normal" world and the people who have been pushed aside, put into institutions, excluded from our societies because they are weak and vulnerable or even killed before birth. This gap is a place of invitation in which we call people to respond.[1]

The story of the ministry of reconciliation always begins in the humility of everyday life, with someone responding to a gap. This is also where leadership begins.

It is easy to miss both how big and how small a thing it is to respond to a gap. The gap cries out for people to respond. Yet few have ears to hear or eyes to see. Surrounded, numbed and seduced by the pressing noise of getting ahead and the seeming normality of the way things are, few see that the gap exists. Fewer are bothered. Still fewer respond. Leaders are ones who begin to see, to be disturbed, to go out of their way to respond to the gap. They are immediately out front in doing so.

Yet being out front is not spectacular. Responding to gaps is casual, small, unnoticed. The person may not even be saying or thinking "I am leading." He or she was simply interrupted or disturbed—and responded.

This is why learning to tell the story over and over again is crucial. Chris Heuertz went to volunteer for two months with Mother Teresa in Kolkata (formerly Calcutta) when he was a college student. He had no plans beyond that. He had heard of Mother Teresa and wanted to see what her ministry was about. But Chris could not forget the men and women he saw dying on the streets of Kolkata. He was captivated by the same gap to which Mother Teresa had initially responded. Over the next few years and more visits to Kolkata and meetings with Mother Teresa, Chris helped re-image Word Made Flesh, an incarnational missional community that serves Jesus among the most vulnerable of the world's poor.

For every leader like Heuertz, there are thousands more everyday people who take the time to respond to a gap. In the early 1970s, my (Chris's) parents were missionaries in Korea whose day jobs were student discipleship and English language instruction. But after a student demonstration in Seoul, where they stumbled across a tear gas canister marked "Made in U.S.A.," their eyes opened to the injustice of America's support of the dictatorship.

On Monday evenings, after their day jobs, my parents began meeting with a small group of other American and Canadian missionaries bothered by the persecution of Koreans who opposed the dictatorship, the horrible working conditions of factory workers and U.S. support for the South Korean dictatorship. They gathered in each other's homes to share burdens, intelligence and the resources they had to find small ways of resisting. They visited Korean friends in jail, supported their spouses, secretly channeled information to foreign journalists, lobbied their own governments, even did public demonstrations. For ten years the ordinary people of the "Monday Night Group" went out of their way to quietly assist Korean friends in their costly struggle against injustice.

Responding to a gap is not about starting everywhere but about starting *somewhere*. Wherever we find ourselves, there are gaps. The gap can be as small and near as people in our own family, town or congregation. The challenge is for each of us to be faithful to discern and respond to the gap God puts before us.

Leaders see a gap. They become disturbed. They go out of their way to respond to the gap. This is the beginning of leadership in reconciliation.

KNOWING AND NOT KNOWING

Leaders do not engage or stick to the journey of reconciliation because they feel qualified, but because they are burdened by a gap and respond. They do not know what they are getting into or where they are going.

Eventually, leaders see they are somehow seduced and have no choice but to keep going, because this is the task they have been given. They are willing to constantly proceed, finding their way forward without a grand design. Thus leadership in the ministry of reconciliation is not a matter of efficiency and control. Leaders are the men or women of unclean lips who find themselves inadequate, in over their heads. Yet still they say with the prophet Isaiah, over and over again in the journey, "Here am I, send me!" (Is 6:8).

When Marcia Owen crossed over into the "hood" of Durham to find the loved ones of a young man who was murdered, she was a suburban soccer mom. Marcia had no idea what she was getting into. She did not set out to "start a ministry." Leaders know where they are going *from* but not always where they are going *to*. They don't know for sure what to do next.

Yet there is also a profound *knowing* here, a deep wisdom that is gained about navigating the journey. There is something very significant about knowing when and how to stick with something, even when not knowing what to do. There is no road map into the new creation in Christ, because only God knows what that new creation looks like. The wisdom of both knowing and not knowing is the embrace of a journey into a future that has never been seen or experienced. It is this "knowing" that enables leaders to accept places of hardship where they feel completely over their head. There is deep wisdom in the not knowing, the wisdom of learning what it means to be attentive to a journey toward the new creation in companionship with the presence and interruption of the Holy Spirit.

The further the leader goes in the journey of minding a gap, the more unexpected gifts "happen" to sustain the journey. The leader does not have all the answers, but she does have a story in which wisdom, faith, a compelling sense of call and vocation, and skills of improvisation have been learned. Within the journey itself, leaders gain the wisdom to trust that God will provide what is needed for the next step.

Leading is not about knowing where you are going. It is about starting *somewhere* and then taking a next faithful step, then another and another. Thus one of the greatest skills leaders must learn in the journey is the art of improvisation—of navigating very concrete contexts with the right measure of knowing and not knowing.

BELONGING TO THE GAP

Even without knowing the way, as they respond to the gap, everyday leaders begin at some point to *belong* to the gap. Belonging to the gap means staying present to it long enough to learn what it means to proclaim good news there:

The Spirit of the Lord is upon me,
>   because He has anointed me
>   to preach good news to the poor.
> He has sent me to proclaim freedom for the prisoners,
>   and recovery of sight for the blind,
> to release the oppressed,
>   to proclaim the year of the Lord's favor. (Lk 4:18-19 NIV)

Before this public announcement about "good news to the poor," Jesus spent thirty long years listening and belonging to life on the ground. It takes time for the leader to know what "good news" looks like in a specific gap. The leader stays with the gap long enough to become deeply bothered by the stubborn "now" of it, to be transformed and to learn what good news truly is.

When Bishop Ochola of Uganda's Kitgum diocese lost his wife in a car bombing, he had been working for years to resist the rebels who kidnap children and make them fight for their cause. Together with other church leaders, Ochola founded the Acholi Religious Leaders Peace Initiative, bringing together Muslim and Christian leaders to provide a proactive alternative to rebel violence. He had met with government leaders and with rebels, encouraging both sides to work to end the war. Ochola had tried to change things, only to lose the woman he loved most. An educated man, he could have walked away from Uganda. Instead he chose to organize churches to stand up against the violence and proclaim another way.

In belonging to the gap, leaders learn tactics of both resistance and unlikely friendship, protest and new creation. They befriend, cajole, preach, resist, organize, pastor, protest, console. Their concern for the gap is concrete—food, water, houses, hospitality, bringing people together across divides. Leaders organize people to do whatever is most needed to be faithful at a given time.

Belonging to the gap is shaped by the salvation brought by Jesus, which does not come through a sermon to simply stop us from sinning or to help us avoid hell or to make sure we're doing the right thing. Nor does Jesus promise to fix our lives or save us from sickness, death and all the other realities of the human condition. He offers a far more radical vision of salvation. He came and "dwelt among us" (Jn 1:14) as Word made flesh. That is the good news, the story of God's new creation that reaches a definitive point "in Christ." Leadership for reconciliation requires this deeper presence.

Over time, as leaders are present to the gap, their response grows and becomes more visible, public and pronounced. An alternative to the way things are takes on a distinctive shape and texture unique to the particular gap and its location and context. The leader sees and shapes into visibility a rich externality of what "good news" looks like—something unexpected, deeper and more radical than was thought to be possible.

In belonging to the gap of Washington, D.C., Church of the Saviour has decided that new creation looks like feeding the poor and tending to the lonely. Church of the Saviour's decades of faithful ministry since 1947 have been profoundly shaped by founding pastors Gordon and Mary Cosby. From the beginning the Cosbys envisioned ministry as both inward and outward, a call to intimacy with Jesus and a call to express this intimacy in concrete ministries of mercy and shalom. The result of this distinctive vision has been the organization of small churches and ministries around "mission groups" committed to the disciplines of leading a concrete ministry (some full time, some part time) as well as prayer, worship and regular silent retreats.

When I (Chris) visited their ministries, we walked within a matter of minutes among people of every hue and social class, from the Potter's House (coffee shop and bookstore), to Joseph's House (hospice for those dying of AIDS), to Andrew's House for visiting guests, to Christ House (residential medical care for homeless men and women), to the Festival Center (discipleship training center). There Gordon Cosby sat quietly waiting for everybody to show up for noon prayer. In the midst of all the ministry, all the care, all the swirl of activity, the inward journey remains as central as the outward.

Leaders who grow to belong to the gap are those who journey far enough to feel its deep pain, to lament it, to learn its story deeply. Always bringing the pain of their context back to God, their response grows deeper over the years, drawing others with them into a distinctive way of life. The leader has not come to the place of brokenness for a brief detour but to "offer [their] bodies as living sacrifices" (Rom 12:1).

SUFFERING

In belonging to the gap, everyday leaders take on the deep pain and brokenness there. Their very bodies and journeys become sites of the old and new in contention.

One Rwandan church leader described to us his attempts to build a bridge between Hutu and Tutsi church leaders after the genocide. Out of his experience he named three marks of leaders willing to speak the truth in societies wracked by injustice and to a church that is often silent or complicit: rejection, loneliness and disappointment. In the name of forming a new "we," the leader must accept being seen as a traitor to his or her own people.

The announcement of the kingdom of God and the new creation where there is "neither Jew nor Greek, slave nor free, male nor female" (Gal 3:28) meets resistance in the bloodlines of nation, ethnicity, race, gender and caste. The world does not long for what God longs for. The ministry of reconciliation is a struggle in the terrain of habits, desires, identities, loyalties and power. The gap resists the new, and the struggle is borne in the very bodies and lives of leaders who defy the sacred boundaries. Their restlessness, their being out in front, their speaking of truth to all sides can become a lonely place.

Over time, leaders are no longer at home in the old categories. Their lives embody the journey of reconciliation, and the journey has taken them to a new place. Their bodies are a sign both of restlessness regarding what is and of a way toward the new creation. Their own bodies mirror the cost to God of overcoming the dividing wall of hostility through the death of Jesus. Their

journeys become journeys of groaning, of dying, of loneliness—
a visible sign of the new in tension with the old.

CONVERSION

Leaders respond to a gap without knowing the way. They belong to the gap to such an extent that they share in its suffering. This is as far as some leaders take the journey. But
this is not far enough. While many leaders bear the signs of
the world's death and suffering in their body, engaging the
world's suffering does not necessarily lead us into redemption. We are just as likely to be transformed into bitterness
as into new life.

There are many casualties in the journey of responding to the
gaps of the world. Many leaders end up bitter and angry. They
become despairing and sometimes even destructive.

Suffering itself is neither redemptive nor something to be glo-
rified. It is risky to enter and belong to gaps full of so much pain,
so much darkness, where so much is at stake. It is not enough to
respond and belong to the gap.

The ministry of reconciliation requires that the body of the
leader become not only a site of suffering but also a site of holiness—a site of both dying and being raised, crucifixion and
resurrection. Conversion is the constant journey with God of
being changed into new people with new loyalties toward a new
future. This is what we mean by holiness. Vanier calls it learning gentleness in a violent world. Learning gentleness has great
implications for the ministry of reconciliation.

Many warriors for justice become steeped in the skills of pro-test and resistance. Yet they never learn the equally critical skills of pursuing new life in the gap. One of the distinguishing marks of the gentleness that communion requires is this: *leaders are ones who learn to absorb pain without passing it on to others or to themselves.*

This is what is so remarkable about the spirit of leaders like Nelson Mandela and Desmond Tutu, who are undoubtedly skilled at protest and resistance. While they carried a great bur-den about gaps of injustice, they radiated conviction and not con-demnation, redemption and not final judgment, embrace and not rejection. The truly prophetic nature of their work in South Africa was pursuing justice with a quality of mercy that shaped a quest for communion with enemies and strangers. We suspect that somehow their own brokenness stayed before them to keep them in humility; they kept saying not only "Woe to white South Africans" but also "Woe to me, woe to us black South Africans who are in danger of following the same pattern."

We see this spirit as well in two of Durham's greatest trea-sures, Ann Atwater and C. P. Ellis. An activist from the poor black side of town, Ann eventually came head-to-head with C. P., a white Klansman from the poor white side of town. Ann and C. P. wanted to kill each other at first—literally. Forced to work together after the Durham schools were desegregated, they had enough grace to discover they shared a deep concern as parents for the education of the poor in their city—all the poor children, regardless of race. As they gradually gained an unlikely friend-ship in common cause, C. P. left the Klan, Ann left her bitterness, and both of them lost friends who could not accept their new loyalties.

While C. P. died a few years ago, Ann continues to advocate. She has never stopped telling the truth about injustice. But shaped by the love she learned in befriending a Klansman named C. P., she leads in a spirit that pursues not vengeance but the possibility of repentance and communion. Somehow her deep pains and disappointments along the way did not turn to desolation and destruction.

If we see a scandalous mark of mercy in leaders like Tutu, Mandela, C. P. and Ann, we also see a surprising radiance of joy, laughter and celebration. Such fruits offer a striking contrast to social activists, who often project over-seriousness, harshness and overwork rather than freshness and redemption.

Indeed, if the bodies of leaders in the ministry of reconciliation must become sites of suffering and dying, they must also be transformed into signs of resurrection and new life. Their very bodies, lives and journeys come to embody what is powerfully described in Paul's words about the treasure of the gospel:

> But we have this treasure in earthen vessels, so that the surpassing greatness of the power will be of God and not from ourselves; we are afflicted in every way, but not crushed; perplexed, but not despairing; persecuted, but not forsaken; struck down, but not destroyed; always carrying about in the body the dying of Jesus, so that the life of Jesus also may be manifested in our body. For we who live are constantly

being delivered over to death for Jesus' sake, so that the life of Jesus also may be manifested in our mortal flesh. So death works in us, but life in you. (2 Cor 4:7-12)

The need for such holiness in leaders is critical. It is nothing less than the costly, beautiful fruit of a long and ordinary journey of conversion over time.

BELONGING TO GOD

We know leaders by what we see them doing in public. Yet we cannot understand these leaders and their work without seeing their hidden journeys and tactics as well. In fact, the lives and visions of the leaders discussed in this book do not make sense apart from this hiddenness.

One of the most important Ugandan leaders for peace in the conflict involving the Lord's Resistance Army (LRA) is Catholic Archbishop John Baptist Odama. In 2007, I (Emmanuel) visited with Odama. He shared about the pain of attempting to bridge the government and the LRA, being sharply criticized by both sides. Yet he is beloved among the local people. He also is renowned for coming in his flowing robes to sleep on the streets with children fleeing from the conflict. "Have you forgiven the LRA?" someone asked him when I was visiting. "The question," answered Odama, "is whether the children have forgiven me."

There are stories of Odama going to the children on his knees, begging their forgiveness for letting the conflict go on so long. Odama visits displacement camps, negotiates with rebels and works tirelessly for peace. He says every day is extremely busy, full of visits, meetings, negotiations.

"But on Thursdays," he told me, "I am not available." No one can meet with him on Thursdays. He does not go out. That day he spends alone in a chapel, "before the blessed sacrament," he said. There, every week, for an entire day, hidden from public view, Odama detaches from the struggle, adores the body of Jesus, listens to and cries out to God and departs with a deeper vision to press upon the gap.

The public Odama is well known. Yet there is no public Odama without the Odama we do not see. The hidden Odama points to what it looks like to belong to God, to keep returning one's work and vision to God.

The tactics of hiddenness are crucial, because the ministry of reconciliation is fragile and always at risk of becoming other than *God's* vision. Gaps are places of great spiritual struggle where the very life of the world and the church is at stake and thus where powers of darkness are centered. And because the journey is long, difficult and lonely, the leader is subject to enormous dangers, including pride, obsessive work, utilitarianism, lone-rangerism and a gradual shriveling up due to lack of fresh insights and resources.

While the world of the expert is one of external techniques and strategies, these resources and tactics are insufficient for the leader in the ministry of reconciliation. This unique kind of leader must learn to draw deeply from the often-hidden gifts God gives to refresh and discipline in ways that keep God at the center.

One gift is *prayer and meditation*. There, as we stop our work amid so much noise and clamor of activity to adore Jesus, to bring our struggles and questions before him and to be attentive to his voice, we remember that reconciliation is God's gift, God's vision, God's initiative. To be in the presence of Christ in this way *is* the work in the sense that, over time, we and the vision will be permanently changed.

Another gift God gives is *the church and Christian community*. Of course the church is always full of problems and weakness. Yet it is critical for leaders to obediently connect themselves in faith to her vitality and gifts. By being grounded in the church's life and worship and in the unique story and vision she alone holds, we are shaped within a journey, task and community that is bigger than "me" and "my" gap. There is no public Mother Teresa without the one who, until recently, remained hidden. Her private journals reveal a world of spiritual retreats and directors, prayers full of tears and wrestling with God, bishops putting her vision to the test, disciplines of transparency and reflection, and a community that corrected, nourished and encouraged her.[2] In learning to belong to a community, we learn to return our work to God.

Another gift is *theological reflection*. One of the greatest dangers facing work for justice and peace birthed within a Christian vision is the gradual detachment of that work from its unique Christian roots and vision. In the world of gaps—of injustices and divisions between people—the journey can gradually become about external needs alone: building more houses, serving more people, economic flourishing and self-sufficiency, attending to more demands. Slowly the leader and work drift away from their roots in a journey with Jesus.

This story is repeated over and over. Leaders become more and more utilitarian and pragmatic and lose attentiveness to how the Christian story shapes a distinct and radical vision of hope and transformation. This is why theological reflection is so critical, constantly asking the question "Why are we bothering with this work? What are we leading toward? How is this work different because of our convictions about God's love for the world in Jesus Christ?" Theological reflection requires a certain critical distance, the discipline of stepping away from the work for a time to reflect, including reflections with conversation partners outside the work.

The final gift we want to name is *sabbath*. In learning the discipline of stopping everything to worship God, rest, feast and celebrate, we remember that God is the only Indispensable One. God gently dethrones us, and Jesus comes to the center of the work and reminds us that God is the subject of the journey. We can trust God to carry us and to give us what we need.

This interruption of sabbath in a broken world returns us to where we began this book, with our conviction that learning to become faithful pilgrims amid the brokenness of this world is about becoming more Christian. When we learn how to slow down to respond to a gap, when we learn to keep going even when we don't know the way, when we learn to belong to the gap long enough to suffer and to be transformed and to embody good news there and when we learn to belong to God along the way, we become more Christian.

This is the heart, spirit and life of leaders in the journey of reconciliation. This is what it means to become more Christian by slowing down. This is the light that everyday leaders radiate through earthen vessels in a broken and divided world, the light that points to Christ.

Epilogue

Going the Long Haul

*W*e have tried to sketch the journey of reconciliation as a vision of everyday faithfulness that leads toward the reconciliation of all things in Christ. The fundamental measure of success in this journey is the long haul.

There is no avoiding it: the journey of reconciliation that we have invited you into is long. It is difficult, daily work. Protesting and opposing is one thing—and a vital call at that. But shaping beloved community between strangers and enemies is quite a different matter, especially when we confess that God is the greatest stranger in a broken world. The challenge of the long haul is learning to embody God's different vision of time and transformation—a vision that is strange to a world of speed, of confidence in bringing change without God, of peace without repentance.

John Perkins saw the end of legal segregation in his lifetime, but not the end of poverty in Mendenhall or West Jackson or North Pasadena. No one who participated in his beating ever came and asked for forgiveness. Marcia Owen has not seen Durham fall to its knees in repentance over all the violence in the city, nor has Ann Atwater seen the churches of the city surround poor children of all colors with the care that she and C. P. strove to provide. In spite of the clamor about South Africa "exporting reconciliation," Desmond Tutu and Michael Lapsley know that with the end of apartheid and the completion of tasks by a truth and reconciliation commission, the deeper work has only begun. Younger leaders like Phileena and Chris Heuertz and Jonathan and Leah Wilson-Hartgrove are remarkable signs of hope, and theirs is a restless generation of Christians. But the masses of their peers still prefer to pursue the promises of Wall Street rather than the highways and byways of the world's poorest communities.

In the face of the long haul, inevitably the question comes, not only once, but over and over in the journey: Why bother? Given the difficulties of the gaps and the resistance in ourselves and others to the new creation, why bother?

"For the joy set before him," the Scriptures tell us, "[Jesus] endured the cross" (Heb 12:2). For us to live as if reconciliation is God's work, the long haul must eventually become marked by the pursuit of joy, not merely dogged discipline and duty. Without a spirit of joy, not only is the pursuit of peace not worth the difficulty and unsustainable over the long haul, but there may be something even more deeply flawed.

Epilogue

At stake is a summons to see reconciliation not merely as a challenge of what "ought" and "should" be done but as an invitation from God to participate in what is most beautiful and true. And what is most beautiful and true? The journey with companions toward God's new creation—through the holes of Calcutta, the gaps of Durham, the divides of northern Uganda, the challenges of post-civil-rights America, the fragmentation of our own families and congregations—further and further into a future of friendship with God and others. This is a fragile journey of dying and being raised, of seeing signs of hope break in, of tasting that new creation God has named as very, very good.

Transformation as the deeper vision of enemies and strangers becoming friends—and of all becoming God's companions—takes time. A long time. More time than we have. The work is never done in our lifetime. We never arrive. We never fix it all. God's work of forming this new community of friendship in the world happens in this fragile "time between the times," between the resurrection of Jesus and his return.

Here and now, in the meantime, we take the time to do it well. In the meantime, we go into the gaps and lay down our lives. We choose to go far and not fast, taking the time to travel with companions. We do what we can by giving what we have, with love and excellence, even if our best is given to those things that seem small. For we have learned the significance of washing the feet of the one who will betray us and of going out of our way for the stranger by the side of the road. And surely we will take enough time so as not to lose those nearest to us along the way. For what message of global peace do we have if we are not seen as people of peace by those nearest to us, who know us best, who see us every day—our children, our spouses, our loved ones, our neighbors and coworkers?

You go to the gap because you should. But you keep going because you and others have come to know Jesus more intimately along the way. You have come to see that you and the world are deprived and diminished apart from the stranger. Eventually you look back and realize that even amid all the challenges, there are many signs of hope and glimpses of glory. You find that God has surprised you and your companions over and over with all that you needed to go on, that you and others have somehow become new people in the gaps.

What we learn in all this, and proclaim through our living, is that what matters for faithfulness in reconciliation is not the moment or the big splash but who we become with others over the long haul and what we leave behind with them. And what is at the same time small and yet so very much to leave behind is this: a footprint in a broken world that proclaims, "The way things are is not the way things have to be."

At the end of our days, when we have left such a footprint and lived by God's time with the time we have, when the words come from the Lord God, who brought the world into being and who raised Jesus from the dead, those words, too, are enough for us: "Well done, good and faithful servant."

And that, fellow pilgrim, is success.

Recovering Reconciliation
as the Mission of God

Ten Theses

1. *Reconciliation is God's gift to the world. Healing of the world's deep brokenness does not begin with us and our action, but with God and God's gift of new creation.* When we neglect the story of God's life and action, reconciliation may become popular, but its content will always remain vague. Christians often try to fix the brokenness of the world in a way that puts either us or the world at the center. In responding to the urgent needs of the world, our first question ought not be "what should we do?" but rather "what is going on?" The story of our lives and the story of the world begin with what God has already accomplished. The center of that story is Jesus Christ—

"Therefore, if anyone is in Christ, the new creation has come. . . . God was reconciling the world to himself in Christ" (2 Cor 5:17, 19 TNIV). When reconciliation is connected to God's story and life, the invitation to be ambassadors of God's reconciliation in the world is made clear and urgent.

2. Reconciliation is not a theory, achievement, technique or event. It is a journey. Scripture is central to the ministry of reconciliation because it both points to the specific end toward which the journey leads and shapes the path of our journey as we engage the deep brokenness of real places and lives. Without the unique stories of Scripture, we cannot cultivate the imagination necessary to live into the gifts and challenges of the journey of reconciliation.

3. The end toward which the journey of reconciliation leads is the shalom of God's new creation—a future not yet fully realized, but holistic in its transformation of the personal, social and structural dimensions of life. A key question must always be "reconciliation toward what?" Reconciliation is not merely about getting along with neighbors or feeling at peace with God. It cannot be reduced solely to the personal or to the social dimension. It is not merely a political end to conflict nor mediation without healing. Reconciliation must never become a tool of the powerful to preserve the status quo. Rather, reconciliation is always a journey of transformation toward a new future of friendship with God and people, a holistic and concrete vision of human flourishing.

4. The journey of reconciliation requires the discipline of

lament. We say "discipline" because lament is the hard work of learning to see and name the brokenness of the world. To the extent we have not learned to lament, we deal superficially with the world's brokenness, offering quick and easy fixes that do not require our conversion. The discipline of lament not only allows us to see the depth of the world's brokenness (including our own and the church's complicity in it); it also shapes reconciliation as a journey that involves truth, conversion and forgiveness.

5. *In a broken world God is always planting seeds of hope, though often not in the places we expect or even desire.* Reconciliation requires hope. But the ability to hope requires training. Hurried attempts at success in reconciliation can mask a desire to short-circuit the journey of reconciliation, revealing our inability to recognize and live with the signs of a new creation God gives. At the same time, it is easy to despair and give up hope in a broken world. The journey of reconciliation involves learning to see and embody signs of hope as well as training to live with hopeful patience in the sluggish present.

6. *There is no reconciliation without memory, because there is no hope for a peaceful tomorrow that does not seriously engage both the pain of the past and the call to forgive.* "Reconciliation without memory" and "justice without communion" are both failures to remember well—the first by forgetting the wounds of history, the second by forgetting the promise of resurrection and the call to forgiveness. A Christian vision of reconciliation provides resources to avoid both of these temptations by remembering the wounds in Jesus' resurrected body.

7. Reconciliation needs the church, but not as just another social agency or NGO. Reconciliation is not the ministry of experts. It is God's gift to "anyone in Christ." Christians learn what it means both to be reconciled and to be ambassadors of reconciliation in and through the church, which is called to be a "demonstration plot" of the social existence made possible by God's gift of reconciliation. The church's vocation is to be an interruption of the story of division and violence in the world, participating with the ongoing work of the Holy Spirit pointing to the peace of God's new creation. Without such interruption, we would not even know the alternative that is made possible by God's new creation. To be a sign and agent of reconciliation, the church must inspire and embody a deeper vocation of hope in broken places. We do this through our presence in local places and in the everyday and ongoing practices of building community, fighting injustice and resisting oppression, while also offering care, hospitality and service—especially to the alien and the enemy.

8. The ministry of reconciliation requires and calls forth a specific type of leadership that is able to unite a deep vision with the concrete skills, virtues and habits necessary for the long and often lonesome journey of reconciliation. We have many experts in reconciliation, but not many leaders. Reconciliation requires leaders rooted in God's vision of the beyond who work patiently in the thick stubbornness of the now. Formation and conversion produce such leaders, requiring not only good mentors but also a lifestyle marked by prayer, courage, joy and practical wisdom.

9. *There is no reconciliation without conversion, the constant journey with God into a future of new people and new loyalties.* Broken by sin, we do not long for what God wants. The world and its dividing lines such as nation, ethnicity, race, sex, male and female, power and caste resist the new creation of God's beloved community, where there is "neither Jew nor Greek, there is neither slave nor free man, there is neither male nor female" (Gal 3:28). Self-interest easily becomes the goal of relationships, and loyalty to one's own group easily becomes the aim of politics. Reconciliation thus requires a transformation of desire, habits and loyalties. This long and costly journey of conversion is impossible without God's forgiveness and grace. But there is reason to hope: God has promised to give us everything we need for this transformation.

10. *Imagination and conversion are the very heart and soul of reconciliation.* Reconciliation is about learning to live by a new imagination. God desires to shape lives and communities that reflect the story of God's new creation, offering concrete examples of another way and practices that engage the everyday challenges of peaceful existence in the world. That is why the work of reconciliation is sustained more through storytelling and apprenticeship than by training in techniques and how-tos. Through friendship with God, the stories of Scripture and faithful lives, and learning the virtues and daily practices those stories communicate, reconciliation becomes an ordinary, everyday pattern of life for Christians.

Acknowledgments

*W*hen we walked along a North Carolina beach in December 2004 to begin envisioning the Center for Reconciliation, we named many gifts that might make such a vision flourish. Naming God's gifts of people has become a regular practice for us, a reminder that God is the subject of this journey. We have received many such gifts in the course of writing this book.

Greg Jones, our dean at Duke Divinity School, opened the door that made the center possible and offers incredible encouragement and support on the journey.

Nancy Rich is not only the chairwoman of our advisory board, but also a cheerleader, nurturer, fellow pilgrim and dear friend. Her gift of hospitality shapes the ethos of the entire work.

Our advisory board has come alongside us and ensured that the mission continues to flourish. Thank you, Sam Barkat, Curtiss DeYoung, Susan Dunwoody, Mark Foglesong, Phileena and Chris Heuertz, Renie McCutcheon and Diane McGehee.

Dayna Olson-Getty serves unselfishly and faithfully in holding "all things" together at the center. Not to mention her patience with our "organic" style.

The Duke Divinity student associates who have served the center keep us young and bring us so much joy and life as fresh signs of hope for the church: Amanda Earp, Meghan Good, Ross Kane, John Kiess, Abby Kocher, Nick Liao, Christa Mazzone, Chanequa Walker-Barnes.

Our friends at InterVarsity Press shared the dream for this series and are a breath of fresh air. We especially thank Al Hsu and Bob Fryling.

Chuck Royce's financial gift made this series possible when the center was in its infancy. Thank you for your faith, Chuck.

There really would be no Resources for Reconciliation books without Jonathan Wilson-Hartgrove, the associate editor for the series. Jonathan's incredible mind, writing talent, humility and daily witness are just the freshness this vision needed. He is a wonderful friend in this journey.

For me (Emmanuel), my family back in Uganda as well as all my friends far and near both inspire and keep me grounded on this adventurous journey.

For me (Chris), what keeps light at the center of it all is daily life with my family. Donna, Benjamin, Talia and Christopher, you are precious gifts. Thanks for keeping it real.

We are each indebted to parents who taught us what faith looks like in a broken world.

Recommended Resources

STORIES

Allen, John. *Rabble-Rouser for Peace: The Authorized Biography of Desmond* Tutu. New York: Free Press, 2006.

Bernardin, Joseph Cardinal. *The Gift of Peace.* New York: Doubleday, 1997.

Neumark, Heidi. *Breathing Space: A Spiritual Journey in the South Bronx.* Boston: Beacon, 2003.

Perkins, John. *Let Justice Roll Down: John Perkins Tells His Own Story.* Glendale, Calif.: G/L Regal Books, 1976.

Rice, Chris P. *Grace Matters: A Memoir of Faith, Friendship, and Hope in the Heart of the South.* San Francisco: Jossey-Bass, 2002.

Spink, Kathryn. *The Miracle, the Message, the Story: Jean Vanier and l'Arche.* London: Darton Longman & Todd, 2006.

Teresa, Mother. *Mother Teresa: Come Be My Light: The Private Writings of the "Saint of Calcutta,"* edited by Brian Kolodiejchuk. New York: Doubleday, 2007.

Worsnip, Michael. *Priest and Partisan: A South African Journey.* Melbourne: Ocean Press, 1996.

CONTEXTS OF PAIN AND HOPE

Gornik, Mark R. *To Live in Peace: Biblical Faith and the Changing Inner City.* Grand Rapids: Eerdmans, 2002.

Kantongole, Emmanuel. *Mirror to the Church.* Grand Rapids: Zondervan, forthcoming 2009.

Marsh, Charles. *The Beloved Community: How Faith Shapes Social Justice, from the Civil Rights Movement to Today.* New York: Basic Books, 2005.

Perkins, Spencer, and Chris Rice. *More Than Equals: Racial Healing for the Sake of the Gospel.* Rev. ed. Downers Grove: InterVarsity Press, 2000.

Thomas, Jean, with Lon Fendell. *At Home with the Poor.* Newberg, Ore.: Barclay Press, 2003.

Stentzel, Jim, ed. *More Than Witnesses: How a Small Group of Missionaries Aided Korea's Democratic Revolution.* Seoul: Korea Democracy Foundation, 2006.

Wilson-Hartgrove, Jonathan. *Free to Be Bound: Church Beyond the Color Line.* Colorado Springs: NavPress, 2008.

BIBLICAL AND THEOLOGICAL REFLECTION

Brown, Sally A., and Patrick D. Miller, eds. *Lament: Reclaiming Practices in Pulpit, Pew, and Public Square.* Louisville: Westminster John Knox Press, 2005.

DeYoung, Curtiss Paul. *Reconciliation: Our Greatest Challenge—Our Only Hope.* Valley Forge, Penn.: Judson Press, 1997.

Hauerwas, Stanley. *The Peaceable Kingdom: A Primer in Christian Ethics.* Notre Dame: University of Notre Dame Press, 1983.

Jones, L. Gregory. *Embodying Forgiveness: A Theological Analysis.* Grand Rapids: Eerdmans, 1995.

"Reconciliation as the Mission of God: Christian Witness in a World of Destructive Conflicts" (2005). <http://www .divinity.duke.edu/reconciliation/pdf/reconciliationas themissionofgod.pdf>.

Schreiter, Robert J. *The Ministry of Reconciliation: Spirituality and Strategies.* Maryknoll, N.Y.: Orbis, 1998.

Williams, Rowan. *Resurrection: Interpreting the Easter Gospel.* 2nd ed. Cleveland: Pilgrim Press, 2002.

PRACTICES AND LEADERSHIP

Lederach, John Paul. *The Moral Imagination: The Art and Soul of Building Peace.* New York: Oxford University Press, 2005.

Perkins, John. *Beyond Charity: The Call to Christian Community Development.* Grand Rapids: Baker, 1993.

Vanier, Jean. *The Scandal of Service: Jesus Washes Our Feet.* New York: Continuum, 1998.

SOCIAL AND THEOLOGICAL ANALYSIS

Katongole, Emmanuel. *A Future for Africa: Critical Essays in Christian Social Imagination.* Scranton, Penn.: University of Scranton Press, 2005.

Philpott, Dan, ed. *The Politics of Past Evil: Religion, Reconciliation, and the Dilemmas of Transitional Justice.* Notre Dame: University of Notre Dame Press, 2006.

Notes

CHAPTER 1: PREVAILING VISIONS OF RECONCILIATION

[1]"Reconciliation as the Mission of God," available at <http://www.recon
ciliationnetwork.com>.

[2]Robin DeMonia, "Preacher's near-death experience," *The Birmingham (Ala.)
News,* November 28, 2007, 9A.

[3]From a presentation at Duke Divinity School, May 14, 2008.

CHAPTER 2: STEPPING BACK

[1]Posted at <www.intervarsity.org/slj/article/1354>. Viewed May 16, 2008.

CHAPTER 3: RECONCILIATION IS A JOURNEY WITH GOD

[1]Public lecture at Duke Divinity School, February 19, 2007.

[2]Theological Declaration of Barmen <www.sacred-texts.com/chr/
barmen.htm>, viewed May 16, 2008.

CHAPTER 5: THE DISCIPLINE OF LAMENT

[1]Martin Luther King Jr., *The Autobiography of Martin Luther King, Jr.,* ed.
Clayborne Carson (New York: Warner Books, 1998), p. 77.

CHAPTER 6: HOPE IN A BROKEN WORLD

[1]For more information, see <www.newmonasticism.org/sfc>.

CHAPTER 7: WHY RECONCILIATION NEEDS THE CHURCH

[1]Dorothy Day, *The Long Loneliness* (New York: Harper & Row, 1952), p. 285.

CHAPTER 8: THE HEART, SPIRIT AND LIFE OF LEADERSHIP
[1]See Stanley Hauerwas and Jean Vanier, *Living Gently in a Violent World* (Downers Grove: InterVarsity Press, 2008), pp. 28-29.
[2]See Mother Teresa, *Come Be My Light: The Private Writings of the Saint of Calcutta,* ed. Brian Kolodiwjchuk (New York: Doubleday, 2007).

About the Authors

Emmanuel Katongole (Ph.D., Catholic University of Louvain) is associate research professor of theology and world Christianity at Duke Divinity School. He grew up in Uganda, was ordained a Catholic priest in the Kampala Archdiocese, and taught philosophy and ethics at the Uganda National Seminary. He now teaches on the faces of Jesus in Africa; the Rwanda genocide; politics, violence and theology; and AIDS and other social challenges. He is the author and editor of several books, including *A Future for Africa* and *African Theology Today*.

Chris Rice (M.Div., Duke Divinity School) spent many years living and working in Jackson, Mississippi, with Voice of Calvary Ministries. He was managing editor of *Urban Family* magazine, cofounder of Reconcilers Fellowship, and convener of the Issue Group on Reconciliation at the 2004 Lausanne Congress on World Evangelization. He has written for such magazines as *Sojourners, Christianity Today* and *Christian Century* and is author of *Grace Matters* and coauthor (with Spencer Perkins) of *More Than Equals*.

Together Katongole and Rice are the founding codirectors of the Center for Reconciliation at Duke Divinity School.

About the
Duke Divinity School Center
for Reconciliation

OUR MANDATE

Established in 2005, the center's mission flows from the apostle Paul's affirmation in 2 Corinthians 5 that "God was in Christ reconciling the world to Himself," and that "the message of reconciliation has been entrusted to us."

In many ways and for many reasons, the Christian community has not taken up this challenge. In conflicts and divisions ranging from brokenness in families, abandoned neighborhoods, urban violence and ethnic division in the United States to genocide in Rwanda and Sudan, the church typically has mirrored society rather than offering a witness to it. In response, the center seeks to form and strengthen transformative Christian leadership for reconciliation.

OUR MISSION

Rooted in a Christian vision of God's mission, the Center for Reconciliation advances God's mission of reconciliation in a divided world by cultivating new leaders, communicating wisdom and hope, and connecting in outreach to strengthen leadership.

Our Programs
- Serving U.S. leaders through gatherings, study weeks, workshops and institutes
- African Great Lakes Initiative serving leaders in Uganda, southern Sudan, eastern Congo, Rwanda, Burundi and Kenya
- Annual Teaching Communities Week featuring leading practitioners and theologians
- In-depth formation in the ministry of reconciliation through residential programs at Duke Divinity School
- Teaching Communities apprenticeships in exemplary communities of practice
- Resources for Reconciliation book series
- Visiting Practitioner Fellows

How You Can Participate
- *Pray for us and our work.*
- *Partner financially with the center.*
- *Join the journey.* Whether you are a student, pastor, practitioner, ministry leader or layperson, the center wants to support you in the journey of reconciliation. Explore our website and see how we might connect.

Please contact us for more information about the program or to help support our work.

The Center for Reconciliation
Duke Divinity School
Box 90967
Durham, NC 27708
Phone: 919.660.3578
Email: reconciliation@div.duke.edu
Visit our website: <www.divinity.duke.edu/reconciliation>.

Resources for
Reconciliation

ABOUT RESOURCES FOR RECONCILIATION

Resources for Reconciliation pairs leading theologians with on-the-ground practitioners to produce fresh literature to energize and sustain Christian life and mission in a broken and divided world. This series of brief books works in the intersection between theology and practice to help professionals, leaders and everyday Christians live as ambassadors of reconciliation.

Reconciling All Things: *A Christian Vision for Justice, Peace and*
  Healing
Emmanuel Katongole and Chris Rice

Living Gently in a Violent World: *The Prophetic Witness*
  of Weakness
Stanley Hauerwas and Jean Vanier

Forthcoming (titles not final):

Friendship at the Margins
Christopher L. Heuertz and Christine D. Pohl

Building Beloved Communities
John Perkins and Charles Marsh